PSYCHOLOGY *of* MONEY

ANNE HARTLEY

HART PUBLISHING Pty Ltd
Sydney, Australia

Other books by Anne Hartley

Financially Free
Debt Free

Dedicated to

My Father, a very special, loving generous man. I love you, Dad.

The Psychology of Money

First published in Australia in 1995 by Hart Publishing Pty Ltd

Copyright © Anne Hartley 1995

All rights reserved. No part of this publication may be reproduced, stored in a retrieval system, transmitted in any form or by any means, electronic, mechanical, photocopying, recording or otherwise, without the prior written permission of the publisher.

National Library of Australia
Cataloguing-in Publication Entry
Hartley, Anne, 1946 –
    The Psychology of Money.
    Bibliography.
    ISBN 0 646 24076 5
    1. Money – Psychological aspects. 2. Wealth – Psychological aspects. 3. Investments – Psychological aspects. 1. Title.
    332.024

Published by:
    Hart Publishing Pty Ltd
    P O Box 816, Brookvale, NSW 2100
    Australia
    Phone/Fax: (02) 9971 2083

Cover designed by Image Expressions Design
Typeset by Image Expressions
Printed by Australian Print Group
Distributed by Tower Books

Acknowledgements

We remember a point more clearly when it is illustrated with a story. So many people have taken the time to share their stories with me and I'd like to especially thank Dottie Walters, Barbara and Terry Tebo, Peter Fortune, Sandy MacGregor, W Mitchell, Tad James, Burt Dubin, Jim Rohn, Wayne Berry, June Archer, Sue Boult and Pam Mountfield. Other stories have been taken from books that I have read or seminars that I've attended. As many of these people have written books, conduct seminars, or offer other valuable services, I have listed their details in the directory at the back of this book.

I'd especially like to thank Rex Finch of Finch Publishing for his advice and support.

Last, but never least, my daughter Lisa, who endlessly listens to my ideas, reads and re-reads my manuscripts and is always supportive and full of encouragement.

Contents

INTRODUCTION	1
CHAPTER ONE **REACH FOR A DREAM**	9
Why you need a dream	11
The power of desire	12
Desire is more important than talent	14
Do what you love and love what you do	16
Know your motivation	17
Follow your Dream	18
Problems are here to motivate us	20
Summary	21
CHAPTER TWO **GO BEYOND BEING AVERAGE**	23
You need to give in order to receive	25
Demonstrate what you can do	26
Create your own opportunities	27
Opportunities are everywhere	29
Never accept less than what you really want	30
It's not where you start, it's where you finish!	31
The gift of curiosity	34
Books shaped his life	35
If you don't ask, you don't get	36
Summary	39
CHAPTER THREE **DEVELOP A POSITIVE EXPECTANCY**	41
What one person can do	43
Your words and actions must support your goal	44
Forget the how	46
Flowing with life	48
The power of focusing on what you want	50
Putting out for what you want	51
Summary	53

Contents

Chapter Four
KNOW WHAT YOU WANT   55

Write it down 59
There is a hard way and an easy way 59
All experiences are here to teach us something 61
Know your life's purpose 63
Know your needs 64
Summary 65

Chapter Five
KNOW WHAT YOU VALUE   67

Values influence your decisions 70
Are your values in conflict? 74
Moving away from values 75
Why you sabotage yourself 76
Changing Values 79
Ending the yo-yo cycle 84
What we value, we look after 85
Summary 87

Chapter Six
CHANGING PATTERNS   89

Change your mind-set and your habits 93
Choose positive habits 95
Associate pain with your old habits 97
Changing your personal history 98
Time Line Therapy™ 99
Forgiveness 102
Secondary Gain 102
Summary 103

Contents

Chapter Seven   105
LIFE IS WHAT YOU MAKE IT
Your perceptions are governed by your rules 109
It's not what happens to you, it's what you do about it 109
Happiness is a choice 112
You can change your rules 116
Do you expect others to live by your rules? 117
Communicate your rules 117
Summary 119

Chapter Eight   121
TUNING INTO ABUNDANCE
The law of attraction 124
Tuning in 127
The power of thought 130
Gifts can be developed 131
Tragedy led to helping others 133
Changing your energy levels 135
Send your energy ahead of you 137
Summary 139

Chapter Nine   141
HOW TO CREATE PERMANENT CHANGE
Stimulus/response 143
How to change your responses 145
Summary 149

Chapter Ten   151
HOW TO LIVE YOUR DREAM
Putting it into practice 154
The traditional approach 154
My way 155

More from Anne Hartley   161

Directory of contributors   169

References and recommended reading   181

INTRODUCTION

*Success is being the person
you want to be,
and living the life you want.*

We cannot
change
anyone else,
only ourselves.

Why is it that two people can start out with exactly the same intelligence and desires and yet one person will prosper while the other just gets by? Or, two people will come into the same amount of money and one multiplies it while the other squanders it?

I've always been fascinated by people, and I've asked myself these questions many times. For 11 years I worked as an investment/financial adviser. During that time, I met with thousands of people, some of whom had plenty of money and wanted investment advice. Others had little or no money but wanted more. From my observations at that time, I wrote my first book *Financially Free* and started running courses.

Hundreds of readers wrote to share their success stories with me. I witnessed the transformation of many who attended my courses or seminars and went on to achieve their goals. But there are always some who do not change despite reading self-help books and attending courses. So I started asking myself what the mental characteristics that set prosperous people apart from others could be—I define prosperous as living the life that you want, in whatever shape or form you desire.

During my research for this book, I discovered there is a paucity of books on this subject. There is plenty of practical advice on money management and investments but none on the psychology of money. It's like putting the cart before the horse: we are taught how to look after money but still don't know how to create more of it in our lives, apart from through hard work. I also discovered that each person's definition of prosperity is vastly different. A woman rang me one day seeking financial advice, she was unemployed. She said, 'I am 53 and I have nothing and I am starting to panic. I would like to change careers but don't know if, at my age and in my financial situation, it would be too risky'.

Later, when I met her, I discovered that her assets came to over a million dollars and one-third of her assets were in investments that could easily be cashed in. Her investments paid her an amount of money as a regular income—an amount that would cover my basic living costs! However, she was used to mixing in a circle where people had tens of millions of dollars and, to her, what she had seemed quite meagre. According to my standards the woman was prosperous but according to hers, she was not. We all perceive the value of money differently.

This fact was brought home to me after my first book, *Financially Free* was published. Although I was always aware of these differences in perception, they had had no impact on me at a personal level.

At one time in my life, when my first two children were young, I had been poor. My definition of poor is having two cents left (no hidden bank accounts) to last until the next payday. From those humble beginnings, I had owned a couple of small businesses and eventually rose to owning my own investment advisory business. I bought a home, owned my own business, had holidays overseas, wrote for magazines and newspapers and eventually wrote two books, both best-sellers. According to my standards, I was successful.

Some people thought I'd do better if I just made a few improvements. One man wanted to help organise my seminars and also suggested I take voice lessons, presentation lessons, and see a make-over person. His intentions might have been good and I knew I needed some help, but the message that I received was that I was not okay as myself. As I had a young child, I decided it was important to me to work part-time, so I moved my office to home and scaled down my business. Some clients thought my situation was ideal while others looked disdainful. It took longer to win some clients over—sometimes it took sheer force of personality. One woman even commented, 'Well, you don't look very affluent'.

It took a few years to be able to accept that, if I was going to do anything in the public eye, there would always be some people who would judge me according to their standards. For a while, I opted out of public life altogether but positive people and new stories kept coming into my life. Dottie Walters, who publishes a magazine and runs one of the world's largest speaking bureaus, sent me releases of new books from America. She wrote about me in her magazine and other noted speakers, such as Jim Rohn, sent their books as well. I decided that the universe was telling me to get back out there.

The motivation for all that I do is to follow my life's purpose. I believe all problems in life are here to teach us something or to present us with an opportunity. In order to write this book, though, I knew I had to do some more work on myself and learn some new skills. I thought I would never write another book on money, that I'd shared all my knowledge in my books *Financially Free* and *Debt Free*. However, I believe in following my intuition, and I just knew I had to write this book. Through the process of research and writing I have gained tremendous insights into my own life. I am now clearer on what I want from life than I have been for years, and I am motivated to achieve more.

I hope you gain as much from this book as I have. I know you have the ability within you to create more money, in fact to create more of anything that you desire in your life. For that is what we do, we create money—we don't get lucky. We may make money through hard work but I know lots of people who work hard and don't have what they want. We don't have to be super-intelligent or entrepreneurial, neither do we have to know the right people, nor even have to know about investments.

Robert Schuller, an inspirational author and speaker said, 'The fact that there are more "talented" people who are failures and more "untalented people" who are successes proves that talent is not the most essential ingredient for obtaining what you want or being the person you want to be'.[1]

Money or possessions are not something that we own. Everything in life is only temporary—we enjoy it, we use it and then move on. But when we don't have what we want we often spend our time worrying, calculating and analysing. It's as if we get locked into a time warp and can't move on. For me, money represents freedom. Having money means I don't have to go to work each day. Money gives me freedom to explore my passions, to be creative and meet some really nice people. Money allows me to be a better parent because I have more time and less stress.

Do you want to have enough money in your life so that you can fulfil all of your dreams? You can. Wayne Dyer said, 'Abundance is not something you acquire it is something you tune in to'. Remember those two words 'tune in'. I'll show you in Chapter Eight how you can literally tune into your desires.

Throughout this book, I have used stories to illustrate key points. There are some powerful role models in this book. I attribute much of my success to always having role models. In my early days, I didn't know many successful people, so my role models were people I read about in books or whose seminars I attended—they have so much wisdom to share. A wonderful teacher of our time Dr Deepak Chopra, gives a wonderful definition of affluence. He said, 'Affluence or wealth means that one is easily able to fulfil one's desires, whatever they may be. It is the experience in which our needs are easily met and our desires spontaneously fulfilled. We feel joy, health, happiness, and vitality in every moment of our existence.

'To have true wealth or affluence is to be totally carefree about everything in life, including money. Affluence includes money, but it is not just money. It is the abundance, the flow, the generosity of the universe, where every desire we have must come true, because inherent in the desire are the mechanics for its fulfilment'.

There may be times as you read when you think, 'This book is not just about money'. It's not. You may think of psychology as delving into your past and discovering why you do the things you do. I have only touched on that in this book. My purpose throughout this book is to give you a greater understanding of your relationship with money and to show you how to achieve your desires. This book is about living the life that you want; in order to create that life, you need to know more about yourself.

Abundance is our natural state. When you fulfil your life's purpose, your destiny, you will fulfil your desires. If you are not experiencing abundance in your life right now then you simply need to learn more about what drives you, how you make decisions and how to set up new habits that will support your dreams. I could teach you how to save and invest—so can hundreds of other advisers. If you succeeded (I say 'if' because millions of others have the same information and don't succeed), you could one day say, 'What's it all about?' I want to demonstrate to you how you can have more money in your life and, at the same time, live the life you want. What you do with that knowledge is then up to you.

I have a very personal goal for you as you read this book. I hope it touches your heart and soul and motivates you to go for what you really want in life, whether that be a full-time mum or the builder of an empire. I suggest that you read the book through first. Each chapter explores a different attitude or aspect of our emotional lives, so you can return to whatever chapters interests you and work on those exercises. I want you to pick it up whenever you feel discouraged and to use this book as a tool to change your old ways of thinking and acting. I hope that the stories that you read will uplift you, inspire you and encourage you to live your dream—whatever that means for you.

CHAPTER ONE

REACH FOR A DREAM

*You are never given a wish
without also being given
the power to make it true.*

*You may have to work
for it, however.*

Richard Bach

We limit ourselves,
restricting what we
can have
by
aiming for what
others expect of us,
or
placing limitations
upon ourselves.

As I listened to Denis Waitley, who was visiting Australia on a lecture tour, deliver a seminar called 'The Psychology of Winning', I decided that I wanted to be just like him. I wanted to inspire and motivate others. It didn't seem to matter that my throat muscles would strangle me the moment I had to speak in front of a group. It didn't seem to matter that I couldn't write a one-page article, nor that my only work experience was typing and bookkeeping. I had a dream—and that dream would change my life in many wonderful ways that I could never have imagined.

If you have a dream, you have it for a reason. You have the means within you to make it come true. Some people say that we shouldn't get caught up in desire, that we can become too materialistic and lose sight of spiritual values. I believe that in the pursuit of our dreams we have the opportunity to grow in spirit as well as gain valuable skills.

WHY YOU NEED A DREAM

When my daughter Laura was five years old, she had a dream—to have a swimming pool in our backyard. She was saving for a trip to Disneyland but she decided that the money in her moneybox could buy us a pool. She picked up five and ten cent pieces and gave them to me for our pool. She gave me back her pocket money, for the pool. I said we would not get a pool until she could swim like a fish (for practical reasons, but also to buy myself a few years' time... I wasn't sure I wanted a pool). Laura threw herself into swimming lessons with a vengeance. She hated to put her face in the water but, one day, she took the plunge. She soon started swimming like a fish. She could jump off the side of the pool if someone held her hand. However, when the swimming instructor decided the class could jump off a diving board that was more than a metre above the water, she did it without hesitation, all by herself. Even though she said she was 'so scared'. Then she went back to do it again and again.

A pool was not on my immediate list of priorities, but it is hard to resist someone who has a dream. On hot summer nights, we would sit in our garden and plan where the pool would be. Soon Laura's dream will come true. That's the power of a dream. It doesn't matter if you are five or 85, we all need a dream.

Achieving a dream like a pool can be fun, but just look at what Laura learned along the way. Laura knew she had to conquer her fear of going underwater in order to have what she wanted. She did it; she won a victory over fear. In order to learn to swim, she had to learn to apply herself. She had to decide whether she wanted to go to Disneyland or have a pool. Laura learned to prioritise and make choices—and to focus on what she wanted. She learned to persist. Importantly, she discovered that she has the power to influence others when she wants something intensely enough. She has succeeded, and the memory of her success will remain in her subconscious for all time.

Laura gained valuable life skills and elevated her self-esteem, all at the same time. That is why dreams are so important. It is not just the acquisition of money or possessions. Reaching for a dream allows us to acquire skills through the process of attaining our goals, and we can still learn important lessons when something we strive for doesn't work out.

THE POWER OF DESIRE

After young Wayne's family was deserted by his father, he spent a number of his childhood years in foster homes. When his mother remarried and was able to reunite the family, he would watch 'The Tonight Show' with Steve Allen. He would imagine himself on the show, as an adult, being interviewed.

Wayne decided to become a teacher because he liked having

Chapter 1 – Reach for a Dream

an audience. He worked for a year, saving 90 per cent of his income, to put himself through college. He was the first one in his family to attend college. Being a teacher was good, but it didn't give him the freedom he desired, so he became a school counsellor. However, he soon noticed that university professors had more freedom, so he studied some more and became a university professor. Each step in Wayne's career move was motivated by his desire to have more freedom.

Wayne wrote a book in which he analysed attitudes towards success and failure: he pictured himself succeeding and talking to people all over America. One day the mental image was so clear, he knew it was just a matter of time before it became reality. He resigned from the university, then told his family knowing they would support his dream.

In his view, every obstacle would become an opportunity. His publisher held a minimal number of Wayne's books and bookshops did not necessarily have it in stock. So he bought up a large quantity of his books and left them on consignment with the bookshops in areas where he gave talks. In this way, he became his own distributor. Wayne travelled the country, paying his own expenses, staying in cheap motels, and talking on local TV shows and to small newspapers. A media expert told him he should be happy if he managed to sell a few thousand books… and that he would never get national publicity. However, Wayne firmly believed that he could get his message out all across America, if he took the time and expended the energy.

Then one day a call came from his agent. His book was on the *New York Times* National Best-Seller List. Not long afterwards he was asked to appear on 'The Tonight Show', with host, Shecky Greene. The first guest that evening was Steve Allen. For Wayne Dyer, his childhood dream had become a reality.

Dr Wayne Dyer's books have sold over 55 million copies

internationally. In that first year of following his dream he made more money than he had previously earned in his entire working life[2].

How often have you had dreams and put them aside because you thought that you were too old, or lacking in education or talent? Maybe someone even put you down, criticised you (sometimes with the best of intentions), and so you locked your dreams away and got on with being sensible. Now is the time to take those dreams out again. Maybe they were just childhood fantasies, but if you don't explore them and nurture them, you will never know what you might have achieved.

Putting up with less than you want is a health (and wealth) hazard. Studies carried out in America on sudden premature death of people under 65 showed that the majority of these people were cynical, hostile, aggressive and hated their job. They also discovered that more people die sudden premature deaths at 9 a.m. on Monday mornings than at any other time.

I believe that if you have a desire you have it for a reason, and if you don't have the talent yet you can develop it.

Desire is more important than talent

I cannot remember a time when I have not been reading a book, usually two or three at the one time. So for me it seemed only natural to dream of writing my own book one day. With the exception of my mother, no-one else thought I had any talent. They were right—I didn't.

Over the years, I submitted the occasional story to magazines, only to receive rejections. One day at work, when I told my boss that I wanted to write, he said I could start by compiling the office procedures manual. I was delighted. I put a great deal of effort into the task, and waited anxiously for his comments. He

Chapter 1 – Reach for a Dream

took his time then said, 'Anne, forget about writing!' But I wasn't prepared to do that. I knew I didn't have any great talent but I had read *The Power of Positive Thinking* by Norman Vincent Peale and many other wonderful motivational books. I *knew* I could learn.

My career progressed and I was appointed manager of a women's investment advisory group. I was asked by a major magazine to write a column for them, but my employer refused to let me write it; instead my firm had their public relations person write it under my name. I was delighted when the magazine turned the column down.

I began to visualise my photo and name at the top of a column, and set a time limit of six months for achieving my goal. I told every journalist who I came in contact with that I wanted to write a column. One day a freelance journalist rang: *Cleo* magazine was looking for a financial columnist, would I like to submit something? I did, and they accepted it. I still had not undertaken a writing course, and (as you may have guessed) I did not have any great talent. But I *did* have a good knowledge of money and investments, and that is what they bought. Their editors did the rest.

Each month I would read the magazine column I had written and check it word-for-word against my original version. There were considerable changes. So, I took note of all changes, my style improved, and within six months I was writing for two major magazines and two local newspapers. Now it was time to write my book.

I took one day a week away from the office to devote myself to my book. At first, I sat there and said to myself, 'How does one write a book?' So I would take out my favourite authors and study their style. Finally, my book was accepted by Doubleday, the publishing company. I worked with two wonderful editors who taught me how to structure a book, and how to re-phrase a sentence.

That book, *Financially Free*, became an immediate best-seller. My publishers had so many orders from bookstores that a second print run was necessary even before the release date, and they asked me to write a second book. Another publisher even rang and said, 'Anything you would like to write, we would like to publish'.

That's the power of a dream. Never let anyone tell you it can't be done when you know in your heart it can. When you want something badly enough, people will come into your life to help you achieve it (the law of attraction is explained in Chapter Eight). I also learned another valuable lesson—that I could be paid while I learnt.

Do what you love and love what you do

Wayne Dyer said, 'Abundance flows when we love what we are doing'[2]. I love communicating, I love expressing my feelings, I love sharing what I have learnt with others. Money is what I receive in return for my efforts but it is only part of the pleasure. Norman Vincent Peale said that when you find something of value, the greatest pleasure you will ever have will be sharing it with others. When you live your dream you cannot help but inspire others.

Maxwell Maltz, a world famous plastic surgeon, wrote many inspirational books on how to get more out of life. His book *Psycho-Cybernetics* sold over 30 million copies. He spoke to thousands and inspired many. One day Bobbe Sommers attended one of Maxwell Maltz's seminars during which he asked for volunteers, to demonstrate a point. Bobbe put up her hand and went up on stage. Maxwell asked her to choose one goal, one that would 'make her heart sing!' Bobbe couldn't answer at first, but Maxwell kept on asking questions. Finally, Bobbe said that she wanted to be a professional speaker. She wanted to teach as many people as possible the importance of self-esteem.

Maxwell said to her, 'Somebody out there in the world is going to get your goals, so why not you?' Bobbe went on to attain her PhD in psychology. She became an internationally recognised authority on self-esteem. She wrote two best-selling books and became a speaker in great demand by leading companies and government departments. Bobbe says, 'Life is not about fairness. It is about choices'[3].

I'm sure you've wondered at some time why some people achieve their goals and others don't? You may even have said something like the words my girlfriend said to me, 'Anne, ordinary people are not like you. I don't have your talents, I couldn't even begin to think about a business of my own because I know it is not possible'.

For some reason, very few people expect to make money doing what they love. They classify work as something that you have to do in order to get money, so you can have more time doing what you love. Why can't you make money doing what you love?

KNOW YOUR MOTIVATION

We are all motivated by pleasure or pain. What motivates you? Think back on goals that you have achieved; what was the driving force behind that achievement? You may think you have not achieved much but everyone has their successes. Some people are motivated by the desire to get married. Why did you want to get married? Did you want someone to take care of you? Was it because you didn't want to live a life alone? Or were you motivated by a desire for family life, and a dream of sharing with another?

All of those answers may be true, but one of them would have motivated you more than all of the others. Was it the pleasure of sharing with another, or the pain of being on your own? One person will respond to praise from their boss for work well done, and that will motivate them to work harder. Another may have very little motivation to do their job until they are threatened with the sack.

Up until recent times, I was always motivated by pain. I started my own business and achieved a level of success because I didn't want to be poor ever again. I bought my own home because I was finally forced to move out of a rented home that I loved—if the owner's had never returned from overseas I could have stayed there forever. I hated having to move from a home that I thought of as mine, so I became motivated to buy my own home. Some people have to hit rock bottom before they say, 'I'm not going to live like this any more'. Pain is a good motivator and it served me well, but it is much more pleasant to be motivated by the desire to spend my time doing what I love.

The reason why I, and others like me, succeed is because we know what motivates us.

FOLLOW YOUR DREAM

Jack Canfield tells a wonderful story in the book he wrote with Mark Victor Hansen, *Chicken Soup for the Soul*, about his friend, Monty Roberts. Monty has a 200-acre horse ranch which he often lets Jack use for fundraising events to raise money for youth at risk programs.

Monty was the son of an itinerant horse trainer and, as a child, he travelled from racetrack to racetrack, and from farm to farm, training horses. One day, when he was a senior in high school, he was asked to write a paper about what he wanted to be and do when he grew up. He wrote a seven-page paper describing in detail the horse ranch he would own one day. He even drew a diagram showing where the buildings, stables and track would be. Then he drew the floor plan for a house occupying 4,000 square feet house (371 square metres) that would sit on his 200-acre (81 hectares) dream ranch.

Two days later, his teacher handed the paper back, with a large red F and a note that said 'See me after class'. Monty couldn't understand why he got an F. When he saw the teacher later that day, the teacher told him that it was a totally unrealistic dream. There was no way he could afford the horses, the land, or the stud fees. The teacher said if Monty would rewrite the paper, he would reconsider his mark. The boy went home and thought about it for a week. He discussed it with his father, who said it was an important decision and that he should make up his own mind. Finally, Monty handed the paper back, making no changes at all. He said to his teacher, 'You can keep the F and I'll keep my dream'.

Monty now lives on a 200-acre ranch in the 4,000-square foot house that he designed as a high school student. He still has that school paper and it hangs in a frame over the fireplace.

Monty said that a couple of years ago, his old teacher brought 30 kids out to his ranch for a week. When the teacher was leaving, he said, 'Look, Monty, I can tell you this now. When I was your teacher, I was something of a dream stealer. During those years I stole a lot of kids' dreams. Fortunately you had enough gumption not to give up on yours'[4].

Sometimes we get so caught up in everyday living that we put our dreams on hold. At other times, we have tried and failed. We can look on problems and difficult times as wake-up calls, or nudges from a higher power telling us it's time to do something to change the situation we find ourselves in.

PROBLEMS ARE HERE TO MOTIVATE US

Jim Rohn is one of the most successful speakers in the world. The number of participants at a recent Australian seminar he held was limited to 250 people; the cost, however, was $1 200 per person. That gives you some idea of the money that Jim commands as a speaker. But it wasn't always that way. Jim tells this story in his book *Seven Strategies for Wealth and Happiness*[5].

> I was lounging at home when I heard a knock at the door. It was a timid, hesitant knock. When I opened the door I looked down to see a pair of big brown eyes staring up at me. There stood a frail little girl of about ten. She told me, with all the courage and determination her little heart could muster, that she was selling Girl Scout cookies. It was a masterful presentation—several flavours, a special deal, and only two dollars per box. How could anyone refuse? Finally, with a big smile and ever-so-politely, she asked me to buy.
>
> And I wanted to. Oh, how I wanted to!
>
> Except for one thing. I didn't have two dollars! Boy, was I embarrassed! Here I was—a father, had been to college, was gainfully employed—and yet I didn't have two dollars to my name.
>
> Naturally, I couldn't tell this to the little girl with the big, brown eyes, so I did the next best thing. I lied to her. I said, "Thanks, but I've already bought Girl Scout cookies this year. And I've still got plenty in the house".
>
> Now that simply wasn't true. But it was the only thing I could think of to get me off hook. And it did. The little girl said, "That's okay, sir. Thank you very much." And with that, she turned around and went on her way.
>
> I stared after her for what seemed like a very long time. Finally, I closed the door behind me and, leaning my back on it, cried out, "I don't want to live like this anymore. I've had it with being broke, and I've had it with lying. I'll never be embarrassed again by not having money in my pocket".
>
> That was the day I promised myself to earn enough dollars to always have several hundred dollars in my pocket at all times.

You can wait for life to get so tough, so frustrating that you have to change something. Or you can choose to have a dream, one that makes your heart sing. One that makes you want to bounce out of bed each morning eager to start the day. Someone else will get your dream, why not you?

SUMMARY

Dreams or adversity are the greatest motivating forces in our lives.

Choose a dream that excites you, that makes you want to leap out of bed each morning eager to start a new day.

NOTES

CHAPTER TWO

GO BEYOND BEING AVERAGE

There are those who share their talents and make money, and those who are incredibly talented but take those talents to their grave-poor. I want to know what are you going to do with what you know?

George Whitehurst

Life is like a boomerang.

What you give out you get back.

Chapter 2 – Go Beyond Being Average

The average person goes to work week after week for about 40 to 50 years. Their income provides an average life; often it's a struggle to buy a home and have annual holidays. Then retirement comes and they retire on a meagre pension. Some people refuse to live like that and they live reasonably well, but they spend their lives constantly juggling money, always robbing Peter to pay Paul. They may think they are different but there are an awful lot of people like them, too, and they are still average. Do you want to live like the average person?

Opportunities are all around you but you will not recognise them unless you are willing to make changes in the way you think and the way you act.

YOU NEED TO GIVE IN ORDER TO RECEIVE

At one time Wayne Berry owned Australia's largest seminar company, which brought many of the world's top speakers to Australia. During the prolonged pilots strike Wayne's company collapsed. When Wayne started up again, Jane joined his organisation working as an unpaid volunteer. She worked around 20 hours a week assisting on their logistics team, and preparing seminars. Later, she increased her voluntary work to 40 hours a week. At the time Wayne said, 'The average person might be saying, "You've got to be kidding! Work for no pay? Not me! Do you think I am stupid or something?"

'Jane is far from average. She understood the principle of not doing what the average person does. When Jane joined us, she was working at three jobs, not counting the time she was doing for us. As Jane explained to me at the time, she did not feel fulfilled by the other work. There was no passion! As she described it, she was still looking for her 'life's work'—her real reason for being here on the planet'.

After three months of doing this work, Jane knew that this was what she wanted to do. One evening as they left their seminar rooms at around 1 a.m., Jane said, 'Wayne, you know I love this work. One day, I'm going to be the best logistics supervisor in this country, and be paid for it'. Wayne knew she could do it. Three weeks later, Jane asked Wayne for a meeting. At this meeting, she outlined a plan of how she could do more for Wayne's organisation, allowing them to expand. Jane pointed out that this would enable them to increase their level of client service and ultimately their income. To do this she would have to work full-time.

Wayne said, 'I accepted Jane's proposal. She has never looked back and neither have we. After three months of operating under our new agreement, Jane called another meeting with me to discuss a plan that she had for the future. It involved delivering greater value to our organisation and involved Jane taking on more responsibility.

'Of course, this greater value delivered would mean a greater fee for her services. I looked at Jane's plan, agreed with it and, as part of the new agreement, Jane ended up with my $30,000 sports car'. Jane is now general manager of Wayne's business.

Demonstrate what you can do

Since my first book was released, I have had all types of people approach me with all types of ideas. Mostly, they wanted to work for my company or be licensed to conduct my courses. Some sent me beautiful presentations and went to a great deal of trouble to tell me of their previous experience. I met with a few of these people; often I would put the seed of an idea to them, hoping they would develop it and come back to me with suggestions.

Not one person bothered to research what my needs were. Not one person ever presented me with a proposal as to how they could benefit my business, like Jane did.

CREATE YOUR OWN OPPORTUNITIES

At one time, I applied for a position as accountant with an investment advisory firm. I was told by the owner, John, that I had the position but he had one more person to interview.

The next day John called, very apologetic, and said that the last person he had seen was more suitable for the job. I was very disappointed but sent him a thank you note and asked him to keep me in mind if anything else became available.

A year later, John called and asked me to come and see him. He had been thinking of opening a division that specialised in giving advice to women and asked what I thought. At this stage, this was just a idea in his mind, he hadn't talked to anyone else about it. He said that he had been impressed with me at the initial interview and especially liked the note I sent him. He had often wondered how he could use me. He then went on to say, 'I haven't given this idea a great deal of thought, but if you can prove to me that you can set this up, you can have it'.

At this time, I had no real marketing experience. I had never worked as an investment adviser and although I knew specialised areas of investments, I had a lot to learn. But I just knew that this was my chance to rise above being average. I had a girlfriend who taught at a large technical college. I asked if she would hand out a survey to other teachers and some students.

She agreed. In this survey, I asked questions about money and investments, and would respondents prefer to see an adviser who specialised in women's needs.

Fortunately, I got a positive response. I collated the answers and made up a nice presentation for John at the investment advisory firm. I included the survey questions and responses and my interpretations as to what was needed in the marketplace. I made suggestions on how to market this advisory business and what I'd do if I had the opportunity. John was so impressed he asked me to give in my notice to my employer and get started immediately. My present employer's wanted me to work out my month's notice, so I would finish my existing job at their offices then go to John's office for a few hours for training and discussions. I also worked at home reading as much as I could. I read every prospectus on investments (not very interesting reading) available. I even discovered some little-known benefits in some of these investments that my employer or his researcher were not aware of.

Part of my new duties was to present seminars, so I practised in front of a mirror. I then lined up my daughter and gave the seminar to her in our lounge room. I would write out what I would say word-for-word, then record it on a cassette. Every time I drove my car, I would play it. I think I could probably still give that presentation today. I heard of a course that taught interview skills and how to handle the media. It cost about $600 for two days, far more than I could afford, but I asked my new employer to pay for it and he agreed.

Within six months I moved from being a paid employee to operating my own business under licence. I received a lot of media coverage (the course I did was invaluable), and gained public speaking and writing skills. None of this would have happened if I had not seized the opportunity and acted on it.

Opportunities can arise from simple everyday activities. The thing is to recognise opportunities when they come and act upon them.

OPPORTUNITIES ARE EVERYWHERE

June Archer was one of many who suffer from aching feet. Her mother told her that bunions were hereditary in the females in their family. June says, 'So, of course, I have bunions on both of my big toes. Walking any distance at all was agony and my feet and legs ached constantly'.

A friend encouraged June to take up old-time dancing with her. June adored dancing and had a wonderful time meeting new people and learning the dances. 'But,' said June, 'My feet. After dancing all evening, the pain in my feet and legs was excruciating'.

Rather than give up such a pleasurable pastime, June decided to do some research on feet to see if she could make her feet stronger and healthier. She remembered her grandmother talking about foot exercises, such as picking up marbles with your toes. So she experimented with different forms of exercise. After a week she noticed a marked improvement.

One of June's friends had a painful knee, so June showed her the exercises she had used. Days later, the friend was on the phone to June telling her the pain in her knee was almost gone.

June says, 'Looking after my feet has become a part of my daily routine. My feet are now so happy, that dancing is a very pleasant, painless pastime. As this worked for me, I thought, why can't it work for others? Everyone who tried it agreed.

'I decided to write an exercise program using the knowledge that I'd gained. I visited a craft market and found a wood carver who could make me the correct foot-massager. I made up a kit including exercises, massager and marbles, to sell to others, and 'Happy Feet', the feet rejuvenation program, was born. Who would have thought that sore feet could lead to a new business? You never know where opportunities are lurking!'

Never accept less than what you really want

Very few businesses are a runaway success when they first get started; often there's a lot to learn about the business and about yourself. For a number of years, I sold licenses to people to conduct my course 'Financially Free'. Most leaders started out very enthusiastic, knowing all the pitfalls, and the potential rewards, but the majority never really got going. They gave up too soon—that is why the statistics for failed small businesses are so incredibly high.

When Jay's[6] family moved to the other side of town, his father bought him an old car to get him to high school and back. But he had to buy his own petrol. A fellow student approached Jay one day and suggested that he pay for petrol in return for a lift to and from school. Jay Van Andel and Rich DeVos became firm friends. When their school life finished, they decided they wanted to be in business together. They started an air charter service and a hamburger stand, but later sold both to travel the world together.

Within a month of returning home from their adventures Jay and Rich were back in business again. This time they became distributors for Nutrilite. Nutrilite was a food supplement sold directly to the public via distributors.

They threw themselves wholeheartedly into this new venture and signed on other distributors. But it wasn't all smooth sailing. One night they decided to have a big sales meeting to attract new distributors. They advertised in all the papers and on radio; they talked to people on the street and passed out brochures. They booked an auditorium for 200 people: only two turned up.

Rather than give up, Jay and Rich persisted, and decided to diversify as well. They started a health foods bakery and a mail-order business. Not all their new ventures were successful: some they lost money on, and others did very well. However, they still hadn't found what they really wanted, so when their Nutrilite business started to decline, they decided to sell off the others and concentrate on Nutrilite. Nutrilite was suffering internal problems and the founder of the company offered Jay the job of president—a prestigious offer paying top money. After serious consideration, Jay turned it down: he didn't want to break up the partnership with Rich.

Before too long, Jay and Rich decided the situation with Nutrilite was too precarious, so they decided to develop their own product line to sell alongside Nutrilite products. A few months later, Jay Van Andel and Rich DeVos, both married by now, set up basement offices in their homes. With the help of their wives, they organised their future business—that business became known worldwide as Amway.

IT'S NOT WHERE YOU START, IT'S WHERE YOU FINISH!

We do not all have the talents of Jay and Rich. We don't all want to run an empire and we don't all have the same opportunities. Last year, I interviewed Peter Fortune, a remarkable man who has not allowed a major handicap stand in his way: Peter has cerebral palsy. Despite his handicap, Peter has a fulfilling career, has co-written a book, and bought his own home.

However, everyday activities that we take for granted did not come easily for Peter. Ordinary things such as doing up buttons, feeding himself, communicating effectively and walking without falling over, took time and repeated effort to master. When Peter was young, doctors did not know how or to what extent his body would react, so he learnt from an early age to just keep trying. Doing up buttons was a major feat.

'Did you know', says Peter, 'that it takes seven movements to do up a button? You use two hands and six fingers. Thank God for the zipper fly!' He started practising on buttons the size of a plate. 'At first, you can't work out where your fingers are supposed to be. So you practise and practise. Eventually, I learned, and then I would have to start all over again on a smaller button'.

Peter had difficulty walking up stairs, when he lifted one foot, he would lose his balance. His parents would stack telephone books to make stairs, and he eventually learnt to balance. Peter says that, without his parents, he would not be where he is today. They were incredibly supportive. No-one knew how much he would be able to do, if he would be able to walk or talk, so it was a matter of 'just keep trying and see how it comes out'. He was educated at a school for the disabled in Islington, North London—integration was not an option. On leaving school, the counsellor suggested that he work in a sheltered workshop. The counsellor said to Peter's mother, 'Obviously, he has some intelligence. He might make it to foreman'. Peter said to his mother, 'Let's get out of here'.

Peter describes cerebral palsy as being similar to having a

stroke at birth. 'Intellectually, we are exactly the same as everyone else; we just have problems with our motor skills and speech'. He was determined to get his own job and to never associate with disabled people again. He says, 'If I wanted to learn and grow, then I had to take what society doled out, and that meant a lot of bloody noses and black eyes as a kid. It took me six months to obtain a job in a factory, the kind of mind-blowing job working on a moulding machine, where you did the same thing over and over, and never saw the finished product'.

Peter had speech therapy all his life, but his speech deteriorated while he had the factory job, so he looked around for speech lessons; he couldn't afford private tuition. The only class available was for stutterers, so he joined it and stayed with that group for three years. After that, he had private elocution lessons. He changed jobs, became a gardener, then moved into soft furnishings. Originally, he got to put feathers in cushions, but he worked his way up to manager.

Peter came to Australia for a holiday and stayed. He started out here cooking hamburgers on Manly Pier. One night, a mate said, 'Do you want to come to Toastmasters?'

He asked what that was, and his mate said, 'Oh, we stand around, have a few beers, say a few words'. Peter decided to go along, as it would be a social outlet. At one point in the evening, he stood up and said a few words. Everyone clapped, said it was great, then said, 'We didn't understand a word you said'.

Undeterred, Peter continued with Toastmasters achieving State level and becoming President of the Club. 'I didn't join to overcome something, I certainly don't have courage, it was just a decision to try something. Everything I've ever done has been out of a desire to improve myself. Intuitively I knew this was an opportunity for me to improve my speech and communication. Something inside always guides you'.

Peter joined SWAP clubs, a group of sales and business people who meet weekly for motivational breakfast sessions, and this led to Peter doing some professional speaking. He also wrote a book with Mary Le Clair called the *Easy Guide to Public Speaking*. He has bought his own unit just minutes from the beach and works as Community Liaison officer for the Spastic Centre. He addresses corporate lunches, and does TV and radio interviews.

Peter says, 'I haven't done anything special, you either learn to do something, or rely on someone else to dress you all your life. I didn't want to rely on someone else. We take independence for granted, it's a precious commodity. When I was a kid, I would continually hurt myself while I was trying to learn something new. But physical pain is very short-lived, achievement stays with you forever. It's not where you start, it's where you finish, that's important'.

THE GIFT OF CURIOSITY

If you want to succeed, you need the knowledge, the ideas, the inspiration that you find in books. If you don't enjoy reading, listen to books on cassettes; it's a growing market in America and is growing in popularity here, too. If you are not a reader, attend seminars but find a way to study successful people.

Jim Rohn said[3], 'All the successful movers and shakers with whom I have had contact are good readers. Their curiosity drives them. They simply have to know. They constantly seek new ways to become better. All leaders are readers'.

Dottie Walters reads six books a week; Tony Robbins, now a well-known speaker and author, read over 700 books, listened to tapes and attended seminars when he was studying success and continues to read enormous amounts. But did you know that statistics show that 90 per cent of people, that's most average people, don't read past the first chapter? I used to recommend books to my clients. Often they would say, "I bought that book; it's in my library but I haven't read it'.

Jim Rohn also said, 'Some people say, "I struggle home, eat, watch a little TV, go to bed. I can't stay up half the night and read." This is the sincere person who is behind on the bills. You can work hard and be sincere all of your life and still wind up broke, confused, and embarrassed.

'Devote just 30 minutes a day to learning. You want to really do well? Stretch your 30 minutes. All of us can afford to miss a few meals; none can afford to lose out on ideas, examples, and inspiration. Don't miss learning. Think of your reading time as "tapping the treasure of ideas". You are what you read'[3].

BOOKS SHAPED HIS LIFE

Burt Dubin was a victim of child abuse. From four years of age, until his father left home when he was eight, his father would whip him every day with nine lengths of clothes line, with a knot tied at each end. Burt was a normal, curious, mischievous child, but he grew into an incorrigible, unmanageable and fiercely independent boy.

At seven, he discovered his town's library. There were two floor-to-ceiling bookcases of children's books, and every second day he would take out five books. He started on the highest shelf, and worked across and down, without discrimination; he just read everything he could get his hands on. Books opened new worlds, new universes for young Burt but more importantly, he discovered that books would never hurt him. Although he had no role models at home, he had hundreds from the books he devoured. He became a gentle person with great empathy for others. Books were the means through which Burt found meaning and purpose and contentment.

As Burt grew older, his mother encouraged him to steal from his employer—it was 'what everyone did'—but Burt knew it was wrong. He now had role models, the heroes in his books. So Burt made his own choices, to change his life, to be different from his family and peers, and to live a life of service to others. Burt now owns a successful business and is happily married. He attributes much of his success to the books he read. Burt says, 'Those books were a major influence in my life'.

You don't always have to spend money in order to educate yourself; libraries are free and have enormous resources, and they are available to everyone.

IF YOU DON'T ASK, YOU DON'T GET

The majority of people believe that you need a certain amount of money, or at least be able to borrow money, in order to achieve some goals. When you have such a mindset, you rule out other possibilities. Rick and Linda Gelinas did not let a simple thing like the lack of money spoil their plans.

Rick and Linda started a self-esteem training program to teach children how to say 'No' to drugs, sexual promiscuity and other self-destructive behaviour. One day, they received a brochure for a conference in San Diego that they knew they just had to attend: the problem was they lived in Miami. As they were just getting started with the program, they had no savings left, and there was just no way they could afford it. But they didn't let that small matter deter them.

They rang the conference organisers in San Diego, explained their situation and asked if they could be given two complimentary tickets to the conference. The organisers said 'Yes'. Next they called an airline. The woman who answered the phone just happened to be the secretary to the president of the airline. They explained their situation to her and she put them directly on to the president. After telling him of their plight, they asked him to donate two free tickets. He actually agreed, and said, 'Thank you for asking'.

Rick and Linda now had airline tickets and conference tickets, but no accommodation. So next, Rick called the head office of Holiday Inn and spoke to the executive in charge of all their Californian hotels. He told how they had been given the free conference and airline tickets and asked if they could be put up at no charge in Holiday Inn's new hotel in downtown San Diego. The executive agreed, but said his hotel was located about 35 miles (56 kilometres) from the conference. So the next thing Rick did was call National Car Rental to ask for a free rental vehicle. They asked if a new Olds 88 would be okay? In one day Rick, had organised tickets, accommodation and transport at no cost, but they had to pay for their own meals.

At the conference, Rick stood up and told his story and said, if anyone wanted to volunteer to take them to lunch now and again they would be graciously thanked. About 50 people jumped up and volunteered. They had a marvellous time, learnt a lot and connected with people who could help them achieve their dream. They have put over 2,000 families through their training program. They have held major conferences for educators called 'Making the World a Safe Place for Children'. Thousands of educators have attended their program to find out how to do self-esteem training in classrooms[4].

Take a minute right now to dream. If you can, write it down; it doesn't matter if you change you mind as you learn more about yourself. Allow yourself the luxury of having everything that you really want. Don't just fantasize—is this something you would be prepared to work for? Ask yourself these questions: 'What would I do if money were no object?' 'How would I act?', 'What would I change in my life?'

It's not just the big things in life that shape who you are, it's the everyday activities that we take for granted. If you want to rise above being average, you need to reassess what habits you have that support your dreams, and what needs to be changed.

SUMMARY

There are opportunities around you, all of the time.

You need to be willing to open up to a new way of doing things, to take charge and act when an idea presents itself.

Knowledge gained from books, seminars, courses and roles models will give you more options.

You need to be willing to go beyond being average, and never accept less than you what really want.

NOTES

CHAPTER THREE

DEVELOP A POSITIVE EXPECTANCY

We look at what we do to determine who we are.

Tony Robbins

*Your level of
expectation
has a lot to do
with your success.

People
with high
expectations
attract
countless
opportunities.*

So many times I have been told by a client or a friend, 'I'm very positive'. Then, in the next breath I've heard why this person cannot achieve a goal. My interpretation of 'being positive' differs from theirs. When you are a positive person, then you have a positive expectancy. You may not want to be rich and famous, but you do not limit what you can have or can do. Feeling positive is something that should come naturally, easily and effortlessly, if you are trying to be positive, you will probably become stressed out. If your life does not flow the way you would like it to, just put your opinion of what being positive means aside, and be open to other ways of doing things.

Children have wonderful visions of what they can do, it's adults who put the brakes on their expectations. Give a child free rein to believe he can make a difference and just see what he can do.

What one person can do

Mark Victor Hansen, who co-authored *Chicken Soup for the Soul*, is also a professional motivator. He believes that children are naturally honest, moral and ethical but unfortunately, they learn to be otherwise. Mark has a venture called The Children's Bank which lends money to children. Tommy Tighe was six years old when he approached Mark after church one day for a loan. When Mark asked what the loan was for, Tommy said that since he had been four he'd had a vision that he could create peace in the world. He wanted to make a bumper sticker that said, 'peace, please! do it for us kids' and to sign it 'Tommy'. Tommy needed $454 to produce 1,000 bumper stickers and the Mark Victor Hansen Children's Free Enterprise Fund wrote a cheque to the printer who was printing the stickers.

Mark also gave Tommy a copy of all of his motivational tapes; he listened to them no less than 21 times and was particularly impressed by a sentence from one of them that said, 'Always start at the top.' So he managed to convince his dad to drive him to Ronald Reagan's home. Tommy made his first salespitch to the gatekeeper, who then called Ronald Reagan. He purchased a bumper sticker.

Encouraged by his success Tommy sent a bumper sticker to Mikhail Gorbachev enclosing an invoice for $1.50. Gorbachev sent him the money and an autographed picture that said, 'Go for peace, Tommy'.

When Tommy's local paper did a feature on Tommy and the Children's Bank, the journalist asked Tommy what impact he felt he could have on world peace. The boy responded that he thought he had to be eight or nine before he could stop all the wars in the world. Tommy eventually sold thousands of stickers and the $454 loan to Mark Victor Hansen's Children Free Enterprise Bank was repaid effortlessly[4].

If a six-year-old child can have a dream and do so much, surely there is something that you can do right now to achieve your desires. Just make sure that your goals and your actions are consistent with each other.

Your words and actions must support your goals

Just saying what you want is not enough: your words and your actions must support your goal at all times. Saying, for instance, that you want to be debt-free but refusing to give up your credit cards (assuming you don't pay the balance in full each month) is inconsistent behaviour. Saying you want a home of your own but spending all of your income so that you live week-to-week is also not congruent. Saying that you want investments so that you will feel secure, then spending all of your money on clothes is again not congruent behaviour.

Chapter 3 – Develop a Positive Expectancy

It's important to take some action towards your desired goal right now. If you want to buy a home of your own, and for some people that seems an impossibility, you start saving and acting as if your home was a reality. I have found it's not the amount of money that you save, it's taking the action that brings opportunities into your life. You may achieve your goal in the traditional way, or you may also achieve it through other avenues.

Ellen wanted a home of her own in a good suburb of Sydney, but it would cost at least $250,000. She had no savings, was single and earned a good, but average, income. Most people would say it was impossible for Ellen to have the home she wanted, but she decided to prepare for it anyway. She started buying things for her new home, clearing debts and becoming more responsible financially—some time later, Ellen's mother decided to convert her home to dual occupancy and suggested that Ellen buy the other property. Delighted, Ellen agreed, and started researching how much she could borrow and the best interest rates. It never occurred to her that she would not be able to do it.

She had to pay for the building plans to be drawn up, and the local council fees. All of this amounted to a few thousand dollars, and Ellen was really glad that she had got her affairs in order. Her mother borrowed the money to pay for the initial building work and, on completion Ellen bought the property for a little more than the building work cost. This was considerably less than the market value of the property. Two months after the building work was completed, the local council changed the laws regarding dual occupancy, and required larger-size blocks of land before approving development. If Ellen had not acted when she had, she would have missed out on a golden opportunity.

You might think, 'I'm not that lucky, no-one in my family can do that for me'. Sometimes we can't immediately see how to achieve our goals, but we need to be prepared anyway—you never know what might happen. Preparation such as the steps Ellen took to put her affairs in order meant that when an opportunity presented itself, she was ready to take advantage of it. She had said she wanted a home, she took action to pave the way, and she achieved her goal.

Forget the how

Before you set any goal, really think about it. Is the achievement of this goal all that you want, or is it a means to an end? Janet wanted a new car—a quite simple goal. Many people though, make achieving a goal a very complicated process. Janet decided that, in order to get her new car, she needed a job that would pay more money. So she set a goal for a new job, (this is a means to an end goal). Once she got the job she planned to set a goal to have a car loan approved. The third goal would be buying a new car. This is the traditional approach that is dependent upon each step being achieved in exactly the way you plan it. What Janet really wanted was a new car. What if Janet didn't want to change jobs, or her loan application was not approved?

The traditional way allows only certain people, who meet the right criteria to achieve their goals. If you have the right income, a good credit record, job stability and are young enough to borrow money and repay it within a certain period of time, you can achieve your goal. I believe there are many ways to achieve our goals and that we should focus on what we want rather than how to achieve it.

One woman who attended my seminar wanted a car but there was no way that she could buy one. She had been in a business with her husband that had failed, and the woman had been declared bankrupt. Their income was barely enough to live on and, even if they did increase their income it would go to paying off creditors. But she set a goal, said affirmations daily and visualised the new car. Within two weeks she was given a car from a family member who had decided to upgrade their vehicle.

Focus at all times on what you want. Janet could have been given a car, she could have won a car, she could have obtained a job that provided a company vehicle, or, she could buy one on credit. There is often more than one way to achieve a goal so don't limit what you can have in life to only what you can afford right now.

Sometimes you already have the means to achieve your goals but because you don't expect to succeed, you don't do your homework. Helen wrote to me after reading my book *Financially Free*.

> I was very busy, working full-time in our small business, but my real love and desire was in heritage houses. I wanted to own a lovely, big home, restore it and really enjoy the harmony of living in a well-designed old home with all those graceful features.
>
> Our problem was we had little savings (although our business was growing) and we had one house we couldn't sell, plus another with a sizeable mortgage. The type of house we wanted was in extremely short supply in our area. There were only half-a-dozen suitable ones—and none were for sale.
>
> In your book you said, 'visualise your ideal life'. I did—and I wrote it down. I decided that I wanted to own the home and to share that enjoyment with others. There and then I decided I'd like to run a 'bed-and-breakfast' establishment.
>
> I visualised every night before I went to sleep. I used to visualise owning the home, walking in the front gate and up the stairs, but I'd always fall asleep before I actually got inside. I used to say to myself, especially during a hard day at work, 'I already own the home of my

dreams'.

There was lots to do while I planned my dream. I honed my accounting skills and learned to prepare a cash flow forecast and budgets. I found that we had a very successful business and a good cash flow. I also realised, through focusing on my goal and researching finance, that we could borrow against our property and purchase without even a deposit. Interest rates began to tumble, and it was a buyer's market. It was only a matter of time.

I shared my dream with others. One friend tipped me off that a particular, much-admired house might become available. A real estate agent who was aware of our dreams let me know about it as soon as the owner decided to sell. In fact, the house was never advertised. It never even made the agent's front window.

The house was perfect! We negotiated the price right down. I had already applied to the bank for finance, and it was pre-approved. The financial planning really paid off. I had the approval in writing, and this really helped us get the price down to what we could afford. The owner was in a desperate hurry to sell, and it was all tied up in one day. What a day!

All this happened, I believe, because I focused on *what I wanted, not the how*. Now it looks as though I will be able to indulge my passion for decorating and get paid for it, too! We can afford the repayments, and we'll be well on the way to owning three houses and two businesses.

A few years ago, I never thought I'd be doing all this. An added bonus is that my interest in old houses and my involvement in a local heritage group has helped to preserve the character of our town.

FLOWING WITH LIFE

I believe that there is a purpose behind everything we do. When we flow with that purpose, struggle becomes a thing of the past. Opportunities open up, ideas flow, and people come into your life to help you achieve your dream. Sometimes God's dream for you is bigger than you ever imagined.

Chapter 3 – Develop a Positive Expectancy

Someone asked Sue Boult to let them know when some personal growth workshops were being held in New Zealand. This gave Sue the idea to put together a two-page newsletter listing the seminars and workshops being held in the Auckland area. She thought it would take her about one day a week. A few months later, the first copy of the newsletter was distributed to health food shops around New Zealand. Sue says, 'It didn't seem to matter that we were a bit rough-and-ready. After all, I'd had no publishing experience. People in the field were happy to help, and my experience took a quantum leap with each issue'.

By February of the following year Sue and her husband Adrian, were printing 40,000 copies. During the winter, they regularly offered talks in their home and sometimes 50 people would cram into their lounge room. Later on, they decided to sell a few tapes and books on the same subjects. Through word of mouth they had so many people calling at their home they decided to offer these tapes and books by mail order. Sue says:

> I remember one day someone came to visit me at home. The downstairs shop was full, the kitchen was full of people having coffee, the dining room was busy with people working on the newsletter, someone was in the lounge room. I had to talk to my visitor in the garage—I didn't think it was appropriate to see him in the bedroom!
>
> That convinced us to move the business out of the home. The next day we found the perfect premises and had set up shop within 10 days.
>
> The following month, I realised that it was all more than I could cope with. I decided to sell the shop and concentrate on the newsletter which had been transformed into a magazine. The morning on which I was to collect the papers from the lawyer to sign for the sale of the shop, my husband Adrian was retrenched. He was given a large payout, so we took it as a sign that he was meant to help me.

Sue and Adrian decided to upgrade the magazine, put a glossy cover on it, and sell it through newsagents, bookshops and supermarkets. Within fifteen months the premises they were renting had reached stretching point, and they were seeking even larger premises. They had a staff of seven. In just four years, from a dream of working one day a week, Sue and her husband were working from early in the morning, seven days a week. Sue says, 'Both businesses were expanding so fast, we sometimes felt like ducks, trying to appear calm on the top, whilst paddling furiously under the water'.

Since then, Sue and Adrian have sold both businesses and moved to five acres in a rural area half-an-hour outside Auckland. They are currently building chalets that they will rent out as bed-and-breakfast accommodation (details at the end of the book). 'What's important, ' says Sue, 'Is that Adrian and I are now enjoying the fruits of our labour'.

THE POWER OF FOCUSING
ON WHAT YOU WANT

Successful people focus on what they want, not the problems surrounding them, or how to achieve their goals. When you put all of your energy into a project, you emit electromagnetic vibrations that others unconsciously tune in to, this is how you attract people and opportunities into your life that can assist in fulfilling your desires (see Chapter Eight).

Anita always knew that her husband, Gordon, was an adventurer and a dreamer. One day, he announced that he wanted to take off for two years to fulfil a dream—to ride a horse from Buenos Aires to New York! Anita would be left to care for their two small children, aged six and four. Her first priority was to find some way to make a living that would allow her to work nine to five. She decided on a shop; she sat down with Gordon and told him she wanted to sell skin care products and cosmetics, using natural products. They borrowed $10,000 from the bank, and Gordon made up a budget and calculated Anita would need to make $750 a week from the shop to survive.

Everything was done on a shoestring. The cheapest bottles available were the ones used by hospitals to collect urine samples, but they were still too expensive for Anita to purchase enough for her stock supply. So she decided to recycle: customers would bring back their containers for a refill. Anita's main concern was to make the all-important $750 a week. Some weeks she would fall short, so she would open on Sundays or take products out in the van to try to sell to schools, colleges and anyone who would listen. Most weeks she made around $375. She decided to open a second shop in order to reach a bigger market and went back to the bank, but they refused a second loan. Finally, a friend who worked part-time in the shop said her boyfriend, Ian McGlinn, had some spare cash. When Anita approached him, Ian agreed to lend the money in return for a half-share in the business. Anita worked even harder, putting all her energy into her business and soon began to make the $750 a week.

Fifteen years later, Anita and Gordon Roddick had achieved international success with their chain of shops, *The Body Shop*. Anita has written about her achievements in her book, *Body and Soul*[7]. At last count, Ian McGlinn's $10,000 investment was worth $350 million.

PUTTING OUT FOR WHAT YOU WANT

Often when there is no obvious way to achieve their goals I will say to people, 'Put it out there and see what happens'. Sometimes that means telling people who can help them, but at other times it means visualising, maybe affirming (visualisation and affirmations are covered in my book *Financially Free*) so that the electromagnetic signals that they transmit can be picked up by others.

I think this is one of the hardest thing for some people to accept. I remember one couple who came to see me, the wife had read my book *Financially Free*, the husband hadn't. They wanted to renovate their home, buy a new car, have a holiday, buy baby furniture (the baby was due in six months), and start up a business that the woman could run from home after the baby was born. They had limited funds and wanted to achieve all of these goals before the baby was due.

They could achieve some of their goals by practical means but not all of them, at least, in no obvious way. They were not prepared to compromise or wait, so I told them to 'put it out' and start renovating, as this was the biggest expense and they had enough money for that.

I explained my method for goal-setting (this is explained in greater detail in my book *Financially Free*). Briefly, this means you set one goal a month, visualise and affirm it on a daily basis, and do whatever is necessary on a practical level. At the end of one month, move on to a new goal. This method works for me and for many others.

At the end of the consultation, the man said, 'Well, I was expecting something else. I thought you would be more specific, give us more practical advice as to how we can achieve our goals'. I can't make money where there is none; practical planning is important but there are limits as to how far savings can be stretched. It's not always easy to step out in faith, but if there is no other way to achieve your goal, what do you have to lose?

SUMMARY

Set a goal.

Ensure that your words and actions support your goal.

Focus on what you want not how to get it.

If you need help, ask for it.

NOTES

CHAPTER FOUR

KNOW WHAT YOU WANT

*Learning is the beginning of wealth.
Learning is the beginning of health.
Learning is the beginning of
spirituality.
Searching and learning is where
the miracle process all begins.
Formal education will
make you a living;
Self-education will make you a fortune.*

Jim Rohn

*Know
what
you want
and
refuse
to accept
anything less.*

Wouldn't it be wonderful if we all knew exactly what we wanted all of the time? Life isn't always that simple, but that does not mean that we should not strive for clarity in our goals. If you study successful people you will find the secret to their success is in the questions that they ask. Asking questions is great, but you have to ask the right questions in order to get the right answers. If you ask yourself questions like: 'Why does this always happen to me?', 'What am I doing wrong?' and 'How come other people get rich and I can't?' you are asking the wrong questions. Your focus is on the problem and these questions imply that someone is to blame.

In late 1994, I attended a seminar in which Wayne Dyer was one of the speakers. At that seminar, I heard one phrase that changed my life forever. Wayne Dyer said, 'Everything in your life is perfect exactly as it is right now'. Wayne went on to explain that we choose all experiences in our life in order to learn lessons.

At that time, my life was not perfect. I had given up investment advice the previous year to start a magazine. While the magazine was successful in terms of readership, it was not successful financially. Eventually, I had to close it down. For months I'd been in limbo. I'd written another book and, although I hadn't had any definite refusals, no-one was clamouring at my door to publish it. I tried writing for magazines and was accepted by one, only to have them change their mind at the last minute. After all my previous success, nothing was working for me. I knew I wanted to make my living as a writer but the money was not forthcoming. When something goes wrong, the natural reaction is to blame someone a person, the government, or the economy, I tend to blame myself. I asked myself constantly, 'What am I doing wrong?' and 'Am I blocking my own prosperity?'

After attending that seminar, I reflected on the past year. I decided there were a few people I needed to forgive and realised that I could be kinder to myself. I gave myself permission to take a few months off and trust that the universe (you may prefer to call this higher power God, higher self—it's all the same), would support me while I sorted out what I wanted to do. I believe that if we are following our life's purpose, we will always be supported.

Once I relaxed, I discovered that taking time out was the best thing I'd done in years. In some measure, I believe these problems arose so that I could take time out, something I'd been saying I wanted to do but never had the courage to. Sometimes when you have asked questions, you need some quiet time to listen to the answers. I find it hard to sit back and do nothing. One day, though, I was sitting on my verandah, discussing ideas for a business with my eldest daughter, when I said, 'But I don't know where I will find the money'. Just then, Lisa looked into the sky and saw a skywriter, and said, 'What is that plane writing?'. The message written in the sky (I believe just for me) was 'TRUST'—and that's what I decided to do.

I now feel clearer in what I want to do than I have been in years. This clarity enabled me to recognise that what I had been teaching in my *'Financially Free'* program, while still valid, was not complete.

I reviewed the book that I had written (but had not yet published). I decided there was more work to be done and to combine some of the stories from that book with this one. If it had not been for those problems, and the time I took out to work them through, The Psychology of Money would never have been written.

Problems are merely lessons to be learned (or opportunities waiting to be born). We can heed the lesson, or we can resist it.

WRITE IT DOWN

Sometimes we do know what we want but are too lazy to put the time and effort into being specific and writing it down. At the beginning of the year I called a family meeting with my two daughters (age 26 and six). The eldest one has been drifting for a while and the youngest needs to establish some good habits. I suggested that we all set our goals for the next 12 months, write them down, and put them on the noticeboard so that we can stay focused throughout the year. There were some moans and groans at first. They didn't know what they wanted initially but, once they got into it, they surprised me with some very specific desires.

Laura, my six-year-old, wanted more friends—six girlfriends to be exact. She had had a difficult year in first class, with very few friends, so I encouraged her to visualise herself playing with new friends. What a difference! Laura has gone from a child who had no-one to play with, to one who is constantly inviting new people over, previously, she had been too shy. A new child moved in next door and they instantly clicked. We also made friends with another child who lives a few doors away, and now I have a child who plays so much she is exhausted, but very happy. There is a glow and confident air about Laura that did not exist before she took the time to write it down.

THERE IS A HARD WAY AND AN EASY WAY

As I mentioned earlier, Wayne Berry ran Australia's largest and most successful seminar business until 1989, when the airline pilots' strike put him out of business virtually overnight. He fell into the depths of despair, as a result, his marriage failed.

Friends had suggested, before the collapse of his business and afterwards, that he attend a seminar on money attitudes but he kept refusing. Wayne says:

> I found myself trotting out the same old excuses. Then I caught myself in the middle of a lie. I was now far from successful. I had a failed business, no money, terrible relationships and plenty of time on my hands. I decided to check it out.
>
> I went to the local organisers (of the 'Money and You' seminars). I was highly sceptical. I was looking for some good reasons not to attend. In the end, they made it impossible for me not to. Over the months that followed the organisers, Jane Wilson and Stan Jordan, became two of my closest friends and I will be forever grateful to them for convincing me to invest the time to attend. It was a major turning point in my economic recovery.
>
> It also dawned on me that had I not been so clever, had I not be so close-minded to personal development (pretty stupid for someone in the personal development business), I would probably have attended this seminar three years earlier. It may well have saved me two million dollars, my marriage and a lot of pain and grief.

Wayne is now back in the seminar business and attends many seminars a year in Australia and overseas. He says, 'When you hear yourself saying, "I don't need that, I already know everything I need to know about that" watch out. This is a major signal you may already be in danger'.

Sometimes things don't go according to our timetable because there are lessons that we need to learn. Lessons that are vital to our future success.

All experiences are here to teach us something

Barbara and Terry Tebo lived what they described as 'an idyllic lifestyle'. They had bought a four-hundred-year-old cottage in rural Somerset, four-and-a-half hours out of London. They grew their own vegetables, kept bees, had paid out their mortgage and had high salaries. Then Barbara got sick with glandular fever that kept recurring, year after year. Doctors couldn't help and eventually they turned to homeopathy, which provided the cure.

Barbara and Terry naturally became interested in alternative medicine which led them to study and practise meditation. After some years, when an opportunity arose for them to teach personal growth seminars in Australia, they felt intuitively able to leave security behind and accept this new opportunity.

By now, Barbara and Terry had two children, Molly and Josie, aged four and two. But what they had hoped would be a golden opportunity did not work out. After a year of rigourous training, they were sent to Wellington, New Zealand but three months later they were fired. By now they had no money, no work permits and no income.

Their luck seemed to change when they were invited to start a personal growth division of an existing corporate training business in Australia. They had three months to make it work. But there was only enough money to pay one salary and, not able to pay their way they lost their jobs again. They realised that they had had unrealistic expectations of what they could achieve within such a limited time frame. On Terry's forty-fifth birthday, they walked into their local social security office and registered for unemployment. This paid about half the rent they were committed to, and they didn't know how they would buy food. Following their belief that 'what you give out comes back', they started tithing (giving away) 10 per cent of their unemployment benefits.

All the prospective employers they applied to for work said Barbara and Terry were over-qualified. So they sat down and wrote their first seminar, 'Free to be Me'. They started teaching in their living room as they didn't have the money to hire a venue, and sometimes they only had two or four people in a class.

However, within a short period of time, they were able to give up unemployment benefits. After six months, they had $3,000 in the bank. Terry remembers, 'Each day I had to go out to get photocopies of notes for the evening's class. It was particularly frustrating if we were only one copy short. So we decided to invest in a photocopier. Guess what it cost? $3,000! Spending all our savings was scary but it taught us detachment'.

Barbara says, 'Whatever we have now, if we lose it, it would hurt—but it wouldn't be the end of it all. We use and enjoy everything but don't believe we own anything. The universe owns it and we use it before passing it on to someone else. When you get too frightened about losing something you put a lot of energy into protecting it'.

Barbara and Terry believe that they needed to experience poverty, fear and insecurity before they could effectively teach others how to handle these problems. With the insight their experiences had given them and their good training and teaching backgrounds, Barbara and Terry were able to offer exceptional courses. The number of courses they offered grew as did the numbers attending them. Barbara says, 'We went from the dole to owning a half-million-dollar home in five years'.

Know your life's purpose

I believe that we all come into this life with a purpose and that when we come to the end of our lives, our successes will not be measured by our possessions. Whether or not we have been successful will be measured by the answers we give to these questions: 'Did I love enough?', 'Did I learn my lessons?' and 'Did I give something back?'

To the business world, Steve Alexander was a success. As marketing director with a large financial services group, he helped to take his company from an annual income of two million a year to over 20 million a year. But Steve didn't feel fulfilled. He said, 'You set a career goal to where to want to go and you achieve it. Then you think, "Is this all there is?" The company I worked for was sold and by that time I was ready to get out of corporate life. I didn't know what I wanted to do exactly but people fascinated me. I used to wonder why some people would join the company with all the right attributes to succeed, but never got going'.

Around this time, Steve's partner, Debbie, had health problems. Conventional medicine and exploratory surgery had not helped, so they started exploring alternative medicine and they consulted a kinesiologist. Kinesiology is a form of muscle testing that allows you to uncover the emotional problems, that cause the illness, without trauma. Debbie's health improved dramatically.

Steve said, 'I was sceptical at first but I kept investigating. I'd had a back problem for years that the doctors couldn't fix. Using kinesiology my back was fixed and I have not had any trouble since. Everything I investigated worked, I was fascinated'. Steve went on to study a whole range of subjects and eventually became an accredited kinesiologist. It was evident to him that kinesiology had enormous potential for corporations, who could use it to reduce stress in executives. Steve said, 'I knew that executives would be sceptical, but no-one was more sceptical than I had been. I expected it. I was drawn down this path and I can communicate with businessmen in a way that they can relate to'. Nowadays, Steve regularly conducts workshops in stress control for executives, using kinesiology.

He says, 'This is where I want to be. I no longer need to keep accumulating for the sake of it. I know what I need to be happy'.

KNOW YOUR NEEDS

It's important to know your emotional needs as well. I only discovered recently how important stability is to me. I hate sudden change; I need to ease into a new situation. Although I had mentally planned for years to be a speaker and author, I wasn't ready for success when it came. I didn't enjoy it, and there were times I wished I'd never written any books. I realised that you need to prepare for as many eventualities as possible, ahead of time, in order to feel comfortable when they actually materialise. I now set my goals in such a way that I fulfil my emotional needs as well as my material ones. Ask yourself these questions: 'What are my needs (emotional, mental and financial)?', 'What am I prepared to give?', 'What has to happen in order for me to be prosperous?' and 'What kind of person do I need to become in order to achieve my goals?'

SUMMARY

Experiences are here to teach you something, learn from them.

Ask the right questions, ones that focus on the positive, and you will receive the answers you need.

Pursue your life's purpose and you will never have to worry about money.

Write down what you want.

Set your goals so that they fulfil emotional needs as well as material ones.

NOTES

CHAPTER FIVE

KNOW WHAT YOU VALUE

Values guide our every decision and, therefore our destiny.

Tony Robbins

*Be flexible,
as you grow
and learn
more about yourself,
it is natural that
some goals will
change along the way.*

Chapter 5 – Know What You Value

After Dottie Walters' husband Bob returned home to the United States from the Second World War, they thought life would be paradise. They had two children, they bought a home and a tiny dry-cleaning business. When recession descended on the United States Bob could not bring any money home.

Dottie had lost her home several times as a child and was desperate to ensure that the same thing would not happen to her two small children. She'd had to work two jobs all through high school since she was the only support her mother had. Later, when her friends went on to college she realised she was going to be left behind. But Dottie was determined not to be uneducated: she began a reading campaign of at least six books a week, concentrating on the lives of goal-setters and achievers.

Now, all these years later, in their desperate financial situation, Dottie thought of her high-school journalism teacher. She borrowed a friend's typewriter and wrote a 'shoppers column' at her kitchen table, basing it on the ads in the local weekly newspaper. She cut out several cardboard innersoles and carried them in her purse, as her shoes had holes in them. Then she tied a pillow on to her rickety baby stroller with a clothes line, loaded on her two children and started for the newspaper office, her column in her hand.

A big sign greeted her at the newspaper office, 'No Help Wanted'. Dottie thought for a moment, then went right in. She asked the publisher if she could buy advertising space at wholesale rates every week so that she could sell it at retail. In this way, she could furnish him not only with income but also with a delightful 'Shoppers Column' written from the customer's viewpoint. Dottie estimated that the profit in four weeks would just cover the imminent payment on the house.

Since she had no money, she asked the publisher if she could pay him the first week's space at the end of two weeks, and he agreed.

Dottie began speaking to service clubs in order to promote her tiny business, swapping baby-sitting with her neighbour and borrowing a car. She sold enough advertising in her column to make the mortgage payment and eventually bought an old car on hire purchase. She hired a high school girl for two hours each afternoon to stay with her children while she picked up ads and delivered her column to the newspaper.

Dottie eventually built that tiny advertising business into 4,000 continuous advertising accounts, with four offices and 285 employees. Today, she is chief executive officer of four companies, and is a noted publisher, author of several books including *The Greatest Speakers I ever Heard*, and is a professional speaker.

Have you wondered why people like Dottie succeed? Dottie knew what she valued. For her a home and stability for her children were top on her list of priorities and the need to provide these gave her the motivation to do things that she may not have otherwise done.

Values influence your decisions

Most of us go through life without being consciously aware of what our values are. Tony Robbins estimates that only one in 10,000 people can write down their top 10 values. When I have asked people during financial consultations to tell me what their values were, they really had to stop and think. Often they didn't know, or the answers were very abstract. Not one, who sought advice for money problems, included prosperity, money or financial security in their list of values. Yet our values—and you do have them, even if you are not consciously aware of them—have a profound impact on our lives. Our values motivate us, they determine how we are going to spend our time, they control our decisions.

When I first started writing down my values. I listed such things as family, freedom, integrity, honesty, courage—moral values, because that's how most of us usually interpret values. But our material and emotional needs fit into our value structure as well, because they are also the things that are important to us. When you live according to your values, you will be fulfilled and happy.

Before reading any further, take a few minutes to write down what you value. By that I mean what is important to you. It is important to do this at this stage, because your answers could be influenced by what you read in this chapter, and then you will not have as accurate an indication as to what is really running your life. If you are not prepared, or it is not convenient to write your values down at this stage think about them, prioritise what is important to you before reading any further.

You need to take time to be very clear on what you want. You may say that you value marriage but what do you want from marriage? Love, happiness, security? Your value in this case is love or happiness. I know a woman who values her marriage above all else, not because it brings her love (it may to some degree), but because it frees her from taking responsibility for herself. Her husband is a very controlling man and likes her to be at his beck and call. She doesn't want to work, to pay the bills, or have any responsibilities. So her real value is not marriage or love, but 'being taken care of'.

When you know what is most important to you, then making decisions comes easily. For the first five years that I worked as an investment adviser, I loved my work. I used to be amazed that I could be paid so well to do something that was so much fun. I was very good at it and I gave great service, but when I had my youngest child my interest waned. I didn't have the time to keep up-to-date with the constant changes that happen in the investment industry, and my interest in making money through investments dwindled. I wanted to work part-time and I didn't have the time to give my clients the service that I once did.

My two top values were love and freedom. However, even knowing that I valued freedom did not stop me from making a big mistake, because at that time I had not defined my values clearly enough. I decided that I wanted to make my living as a writer (because then I would have all the freedom I wanted) and decided to write an inspirational newsletter. I planned to continue my work as an investment adviser until the newsletter had sufficient circulation, then the newsletter would support me while I wrote books. Sounds good in theory, but it was one of those 'means' goals that I talked about earlier. Remember when I told you about Janet, in Chapter Three, who wanted a car but set the goal for the new job first, then the car loan. That's how most people go about achieving their goals: it works sometimes, but it doesn't always fit what you value.

I started writing a newsletter. Newsletters don't usually take advertising and they are smaller than magazines. They don't have the circulation of magazines, therefore they cost more. So I priced my newsletter accordingly. The desk top publisher thought it would look better in a magazine format and as I was delighted with her layout, I agreed. Unfortunately, the general public doesn't really understand how costing works in publishing—all they could see was a smaller magazine, at double the price. Some people even complained because there were no ads.

By this time, a lot of money had been invested and I had to make a decision. I decided we would become a magazine, sell advertising, increase the size, reduce the cover price by half and sell through newsagents. The cost of producing each issue escalated dramatically because we had to circulate a greater number. In order to succeed, we had to increase circulation and increase advertising. I decided to give up investment advice and give it my all.

One day, I said to myself, 'What have I done?' I didn't want to be a marketing person. I didn't want to sell advertising, or teach others how to do it: all my time was taken up with administration, with very little left over for writing. I'd made the decision earlier in my career that owning a business, with all the responsibilities for employees and overheads, was not for me. I wanted freedom, BUT I felt like I had a noose around my neck.

By this time, we were in a deep financial hole and I didn't feel that I could honourably walk away. My body couldn't cope with the stress it was under and I came down with a 'flu-type virus. It was the most debilitating 'flu I've ever had in my life; I was sick for six months and my life was the pits. Finally, we had to close the magazine down. I had learned some very valuable lessons and one of the most important ones was that the business would never have succeeded for me because it conflicted with something that I valued highly—freedom. I also discovered that if I had focused on my 'end' goal, which was making my living as a writer, rather than being caught up in the 'means' (how to achieve my goal) I would not have wasted time, energy and money.

ARE YOUR VALUES IN CONFLICT?

The most common example I see of values conflict is where financial security clashes with the need for approval from others. One woman who came to see me wanted a home of her own, and a business of her own. She had received around $150,000, the proceeds of a redundancy package she accepted from her employer. Her plan was to take an extensive holiday and then look around for a small business she could buy or start up. Once established in this business she would buy a home of her own. I thought it was a great idea, but I didn't know this woman's values. Even if I did I doubt she would have included 'other people's opinion' amongst them.

This woman was used to mixing in a circle of people who had a great deal more money than she did. She valued appearances, so she spent a great deal of her redundancy money on clothes, furniture and possessions. She took a holiday overseas, travelling first-class, and before she could get around to looking at businesses, she had spent all the money. I suspect that she may have done this in an attempt to find a husband who could support her. If that was the case then her real values are love, security and keeping up appearances. Her original goals, even if she had gone ahead with them, would not have satisfied her values.

So you can see how knowing your values is essential before setting any goals. Tony Robbins once said, 'Your values—whatever they are—are the compass that is guiding you to your ultimate destiny'[8].

MOVING AWAY FROM VALUES

Tony Robbins has no degrees. Although he came from an impoverished background, he dared to dream that he could motivate and teach others to live life to the fullest. He built an international seminar business whilst still in his twenties, teaching people often older than him, how to lead successful, fulfilling lives.

Early on in his career, Tony felt particularly frustrated because his business missed out on his attention while he was conducting seminars. He therefore decided to find a chief executive to run the company in his absence. During the interviewing process, Tony used many of the tools that he taught in his seminars to select a person whose values matched his own. The man he finally chose placed honesty at the top of his list of values. Further checking with previous employers confirmed that this man was 100 per cent trustworthy. The chief executive officer (CEO) he chose did a fine job. The company grew until and it became necessary to employ someone to assist him. The CEO recommended someone he had worked with previously. Tony was suitably impressed by the candidate and the two men, in Tony's absence, jointly ran the company.

Eighteen months later, the business had grown tremendously. Tony was now on the road more, as the numbers attending his seminars had grown. However one day, when he returned from a seminar tour, he was told that the business was $750,000 in debt. It seemed that the management of the company was at fault. It was also discovered that the new employee had misappropriated more than a quarter of a million dollars. Tony could not understand how his honest CEO could have allowed this to happen. When he questioned him, his CEO claimed that he had tried to tell Tony of his doubts concerning the integrity of the new man. However, he said, Tony had responded angrily and stormed off. At the time, Tony thought his CEO was suffering from petty jealousy.

Tony later discovered that his CEO had a fear of confrontation. Whenever the CEO had tried to bring this particular subject to Tony's attention, he had incurred his wrath, so he did nothing. The pain associated with the CEO's fear of confrontation was greater than his need for honesty although he valued honesty so highly.

Although this experience was emotionally and financially painful for Tony, he had learnt one of the most valuable lessons of his life: *that all of us will do more to move away from pain than we will to pursue pleasure*[8].

We all have rules that we live by, but we also have emotions that we'll do almost anything to avoid feeling—and we need to know what these are if we are going to take charge of our destiny.

WHY YOU SABOTAGE YOURSELF

On the television program 'Donahue' one of the guests was promoting his book, telling people to go for what they want in life. One woman in the audience stood up and said she wanted to open a 'fairy shop', but that meant giving up her job (financial security) and jeopardising their home. She asked, 'Should I do it?' The author and all of the audience shouted, 'YES!'

Isn't that what a lot of people do, encourage us to pursue our dreams? I must admit, I do it too. But you would have more chance of succeeding if you know what is running your life. Encouraging this woman to just change course and risk all that she has, without knowing what influences her decisions, what she wants to avoid and what she values—in other words, the unconscious processes that run our lives—may be asking for trouble. There are emotions that run our lives even more strongly than our values do.

When we proceed with a goal, our values can come into conflict with certain emotions we want to avoid and, when this happens we will unconsciously sabotage ourselves. Our subconscious protects us and it will always move us away from pain. There are emotions that all of us would like to avoid experiencing. The degree to which you try to avoid experiencing these emotions is dictated by your personal history. Some of the most common emotions or states that people wish to avoid are:

depression	rejection/abandonment
anger	failure
humiliation	guilt
fear	frustration
confrontation	hurt

Take a moment now and choose an emotion from this list, or any others that you think of, that you would prefer to avoid. These emotions are the ones most likely to be responsible for your moving away from values. Most people will do more to move away from feelings they don't want to experience than they will towards what they value.

If, for instance, you would do anything to avoid failure, then you would consistently (often unconsciously) avoid situations where you could fail. It is only through writing this book that I discovered that the emotion I most wanted to avoid was humiliation. For years, I wanted to be a best-selling author and professional speaker, until I realised that these choices brought a lot of pain into my life. I can remember thinking when I first started being interviewed by the media, 'If I fall flat on my face now, I'll do it in front of everyone'.

I'm not afraid of failing, but I'll do almost anything to avoid being humiliated. I can remember a lot of experiences from school where the teachers would deliberately humiliate me in front of the whole school. My mother's father was an alcoholic and he humiliated his family many times with his behaviour. I remember my mother telling me how ashamed she felt when people knew who her father was. So, for me, humiliation was to be avoided at all cost.

But I also value persistence: I hate to walk away from something. So I persevered with public speaking and promoting my books even though it personally cost me a lot. That does not mean that I am a bad speaker, or that I get nervous. I've developed into a very accomplished speaker, and I love communicating with an audience—I find it stimulating and challenging. But I always feel vulnerable, and know someone is going to criticise me (and they do, some people will always judge according to their values). Over a ten-year period, starting from when I began to give seminars and interviews to the media, I gained so much weight that I doubled my body size.

Our subconscious mind is not the least bit logical, it's a storehouse. Everything that has ever happened to you, everything you have read, seen, or experienced is filed away in its memory banks. At some time I would have made a decision that excess weight protected me from criticism. It also kept me from succeeding too much.

No matter how hard I tried to lose weight, and I did, it never stayed off. I often ate less than everyone else and still the fat didn't budge, because the mind controls our metabolism. I had two options. I could choose new goals that would not conflict with the emotions that I wanted to move away from, or, I could change my personal history, and change the way I perceived humiliation, therefore removing its power over me (see Chapter Six).

I believe that all of life's experiences are designed in order for us to learn something. For years, I thought I had to overcome fear and feeling vulnerable; I've done a lot of work on myself, but I didn't even think of feelings of humiliation, so I had never dealt with them. I decided to change my perception of humiliation rather than give up my dream. Although I knew that I needed to do some work clearing up emotions from the past, I also realised I had to take it a step further and change my fear of the future. Success for me represented criticism from the public, so in order to succeed I had to create new strategies for handling criticism in the future. No-one can set up a goal that ensures everyone will like us, or that no-one will criticise us, but we can change our reaction to it. By preparing ahead of time for future events and what I would say or do I freed myself from my fear of humiliation.

Changing values

I have reassessed my values often over the past few years and have felt very comfortable with them. My values, prior to writing this book, were:

love/family/intimacy	contribution/caring
freedom	knowledge
prosperity	independence
health	persistence
honesty/integrity/trust	security

For me, writing clarifies everything. So, in the process of writing this book, I decided to see if there was a better way that these values could serve me. Our values are here to serve us, not the other way around. Most times, values are the result of our conditioning, and therefore not always what we would choose for the present day.

I had made the decision, based on these values, that I wanted to be a successful author, because it would give me freedom and prosperity. I would be able to work school hours—that fulfilled my need to give my family priority; I would also make a contribution to the community by sharing my knowledge; I'd also be persistent (I constantly re-write and rearrange when writing in order to get my message across in the clearest way); and I would be independent.

Sounded perfect! In order to promote a book though, you have to travel, do talks and give interviews, and this would take me away from my family (my highest value). So there would be some conflict there, but I thought there might be a way that I could work around that. The important thing was that I knew what the conflict was and could find a solution that would fit my values. However, I realised that this career would put me in a position to be humiliated (not everyone will agree with my views), so I would have to be comfortable with having cleared the emotional charge that humiliation held over me. Having done that, though, there was no reason I couldn't set my goal to be a successful author, knowing that my values supported me.

I then went on to ask myself if there was some way that I could change my values that would present me with more options. So I started asking questions like, 'Why is freedom so important to me?' I came up with all the usual answers: I can work my own hours, I can be creative and so on. But I realised that freedom without prosperity is of no value. I could go on a government pension and still have freedom to do what I wanted—but it wouldn't make me happy. More important than freedom was self-expression, and that wasn't even on my original values list.

Next, I asked myself that if there was a way that I could work which would allow me to put family first, to be free to express myself and be paid well, would I consider it? I answered 'Yes'. So that moved freedom down to number four on my list of values and self-expression was added. I then asked myself if I would still write books if no-one bought them: I answered 'No'. What if I could have prosperity and not work, would that make me happy? Again, I answered 'No'. So, success is also important to me but that wasn't on my list of values either.

I also started thinking about other things that are really important to me, like respect. I have never had any real problems with my children because I demanded respect from an early age, and I as I do everything to support them, I believe I have earned that respect. Respect from others is important to me too; if people put me down continually, I don't associate with them. Then I thought about what I like to do each day. Routine is important to me, as long as it is flexible so that I can change my plans if an unexpected holiday or opportunity comes up. I like to know exactly what I am going to do each day. I had planned to work intensely as a writer for a few months at a time, then take a few months off. I thought that would suit my personality best, but now I started to wonder. I need to express myself by talking as well as writing, and most days when I am writing intensely I go for six hours without talking to anyone. So I added communication to my list of values.

I used to love going to the office and seeing clients each day. I still had freedom because I could always rearrange my schedule if something special arose. As I kept on asking myself questions my whole list of values, with the exception of family, changed, as did their order of priority. Freedom, the value that I placed highest of all, and the one that influenced all of my career decisions, was eventually eliminated because, by fulfilling all of my new values I automatically had freedom. So my career choices took on a whole new dimension; writing was still important to me, but I now knew that it would not fulfil all of my needs.

My ten highest values are:

love/family/intimacy	success
self-expression/communication	respect
prosperity	stability/flexible routine
health	honesty/trust
joy	contribution/caring

When I first listed these values, I listed success before health. I was talking about my three top values one day when the woman I was talking to said, 'I don't notice health in your values, where is that?' I said that came after success because in order to be successful, I needed to be healthy. Oops, I had to change to order of my priorities—health got moved up to number four and success went to number six.

Now this may seem pedantic but there may come a time when you have to choose one value over another. The priority in which you place them then becomes very important. As I was looking at career options, I thought of combining my writing career with being an NLP practitioner (NLP stands for Neuro-Linguistic Programming and this science provides a framework for directing the brain), specialising in money and career issues. The idea really appealed to me until I worked out how much money I would make. As I wanted time to write and only wanted to work school hours, I would only be able to see about 10 to 12 clients a week. I had decided that I would like to do this work away from home, so I needed to allow for an office and part-time secretarial support. When all costs were allowed for, I would only make a little more than a secretary and I knew I was not prepared to give up three days a week for such a small return. I value prosperity more than I value routine. Each time you come up with a new career option check it against all of your values.

Having all this information about myself enabled me to make career choices that fulfilled my needs and saved me from making more costly mistakes. I now know exactly what I want to do but the form in which I do it may change. That's okay with me: each time I face any important decision, I will check it against my list of values.

We can change our values to suit us, or our goals to suit our values. We are not locked in to our values. We can choose new ones at any time. The questions to ask yourself are: 'What are my dreams?', 'What values do I need to place in my list that will help me fulfil my dream?', 'Why are these values important to me?' and 'What emotions do I need to deal with in order to fulfil my highest goals?'

If you don't know your dream, change the order of the process. What are your values? What work will fit it with those values? Then answer all of the other questions shown above.

You cannot make informed decisions unless you know what is really important to you. Once you know your values then you need to live by them. Most of us respect people who live by their beliefs, even if we don't agree with them. Take each value and break it down. If success is important to you, ask yourself what success represents to you. Is it approval from others? Money?

Recognition? Freedom?

As you continually ask questions and reassess your individual values, you will gain much clearer insight into what has been influencing your decisions.

ENDING THE YO-YO CYCLE

I have been successful, very successful at times, but for many years I tended to have a yo-yo pattern to my income. I couldn't understand how I could, at times be so driven, yet so lacking in ambition. This dilemma was answered when I discovered that we are motivated by either pleasure or pain (as mentioned in the first chapter).

When our values and goals are influenced by a need to move away from something we create a yo-yo pattern in our success. It is not that we don't succeed, we do, but success is usually short-lived.

I had only a very brief taste of poverty, but enough to make me vow that I would never live that way again. I set goals and achieved them but, once I succeeded, particularly after months where I made a lot of money, this would be followed by months where my income would fall below average. As I was never motivated by money I would lose my drive. That may sound inconsistent, that's exactly what it is, the desire for large amounts of money did not motivate me, I just didn't want to be poor. Whenever money was restricted, I'd be reminded of those early days and I would be motivated all over again. This pattern occurred because the major force behind my success was the desire to move away from poverty, not towards prosperity. I was motivated by pain.

Most of my past choices, I realised, were motivated by my need to move away from pain so, in order to have consistency in my life, I have changed my focus to the pleasure success will bring me. I am passionate about personal development, my work is the outlet through which I express my creativity, whilst making a contribution to the world.

I am also passionate about freedom, and money gives me freedom. I am passionate about self-expression, being a best-selling author fulfils that need. No longer do I need to experience discomfort in order to achieve my dreams.

Go back to your list of values and ask yourself, 'Why is this important to me?' Ask that question at least six times, and write down your answer each time. For instance, if you choose independence as a value ask yourself, 'Why do I value independence?' If your answers are along the lines of 'I want to take control of my own destiny', you are moving towards what you want. If, however, you answer that you don't want to be controlled by others, you are moving away from control. Often you will get a combination of moving towards and away from in your answers. That's okay—it's the primary motivation that is important. If you are primarily motivated by a need to move away from something, then you need to change the emotion surrounding that memory or state so that you can move towards what you want.

What We Value We Look After

Throughout the 11 years that I advised on investments, I did not see one prosperous client who did not look after their money. That doesn't mean that they didn't spend it or enjoy it, they just didn't throw it away.

Often we think that when the big money comes, when the great opportunity arrives, we'll have all the money we need. A friend said to me, 'I just have to wait for the right idea to come. One that will make me a lot of money'. Now that might happen but it doesn't bring any guarantees of financial freedom with it. I've met people with incomes of $300,000 a year, and they are still struggling. Value what you have, look after it, and you may find that you can create prosperity sooner than you think.

SUMMARY

Reassess your values: ask yourself constantly 'Why is this important to me?'

Know what emotions and states you want to avoid.

Create new values that will support your dream.

Look after the possessions you value.

NOTES

CHAPTER SIX

CHANGING PATTERNS

*Unless you change
what you are,
you will always
have what you've got!*

Jim Rohn

*Make way
for the new
by letting go
of the old ideas,
and old ways
of doing things.*

Chapter 6 – Changing Patterns

Dan Jansen loved to skate, and by age 18, he had made the US Olympic team to compete in Sarajevo. He didn't win any medals, but it was an honour just to compete. By the time the next Olympics in Calgary, Canada, came around, Dan was considered to be at his peak—he had recently won the World Sprint Championship. On the morning of the Olympics when he was to compete in the 500-metre race, his sister Jane died from Leukaemia. Dan lost his focus; he slipped and eventually finished eleventh. Hoping to redeem himself Dan dedicated the 1,000-metre race to his sister's memory. He started out well, but at the 800-metre point, he fell again and didn't gain a place.

Dan maintained his peak condition over the next four years, and set a new world record in the 500-metre race just three weeks before the Olympics, to be held in Albertville, France. He was predicted to be one of the medal winners, but he finished fourth in the 500-metre event and twenty-sixth in the 1,000-metre race. When they returned to the US, Dan's manager suggested he visit a sports psychologist, Dr Jim Loehr. At first, he resisted but eventually relented. It took six months working with Dr Loehr before Dan was able to deal with his sister's death. From that point on, Dan paid more attention to the mental part of sports.

By the time the 1994 Olympics approached, Dan had greater confidence than ever before. He had recently become the first person to skate the 500-metre in less than 36 seconds. That was a breakthrough comparable to Roger Bannister's four-minute mile. In order to win gold Dan decided to keep the thought that he was already the best 500-metre skater in the world foremost in his mind. He just had to prove it one more time.

Dan arrived at the rink three hours before the race and did all his usual things—a little jogging, a little jumping around, lots of stretching. He did some slow laps around the ice and some accelerations and practised starts. He felt good; this was a positive sign. When the race got under way, Dan was skating well and he knew he had an excellent chance for gold. But as he went into the last turn, he went off-balance and his hand briefly touched the ice. The next two strokes were weak, and he lost the gold by just over three-tenths of a second. This had been his last chance: although many felt he was the best speed skater ever, he would never win an Olympic medal in the 500-metre event.

Unbeknown to Dan, Dr Loehr had flown to Norway to watch him skate. Expecting him to win the event, Dr Loehr was booked to fly home the next day but, following Dan's setback, he changed his plans so that he could assist Dan to win the 1,000-metre race. Dan wasn't confident he could win the 1,000-metre; it wasn't his strongest event, but it was his last chance for an Olympic gold medal. Following Dr Loehr's advice, Dan cancelled the press conference he had planned, and immediately went into training for the 1,000-metre race.

Up until then, Dan had concentrated all his energy on winning the 500-metre race—psychologically and physiologically, it suited him best. He always seemed to lose steam in the last 200-metres of the longer race; he thought it too difficult for one person to dominate both races. In order to win, therefore, he had to change his mind-set.

Dr Loehr suggested Dan write 'I love the 1,000' as often as possible. He put a little note with this positive affirmation on it in the drawer that held his razor in the bathroom, he put another on the refrigerator, and another on the bedroom mirror. 'I love the 1,000' became his personal mantra. Dr Loehr advised him not to dwell on defeat, but to move on to the next event—he could go down, but to make sure he came back up.

The morning of the 1,000-metre race arrived, Dan's last chance for an Olympic gold medal. Dan didn't feel like skating. He couldn't say what was wrong but he felt 'off', and he thought that maybe he needed to feel more tired. He remembered that when he competed in the World Cup, he would skate two races in a row. Although tired, he always felt loose. Dan realised that what he probably needed was to feel loose, so with just over an hour to his event, DAN DECIDED TO CHANGE HIS PRE-RACE ROUTINE.

He began peddalling on his stationary exercise bike, working hard enough to build up a sweat. Then he went for a jog. When he went back to the stadium he still didn't feel completely right, and even as he took his mark something still felt 'off'. As he heard the word 'Go', a jolt of energy shot into his legs and all feelings of insecurity fell away. On his second-last turn, Dan's leg slipped from under him and he almost touched the lane marker which would have disqualified him. Dan stayed calm. As the final 200-metre stretch came in sight, Dan kept his focus, concentrating on keeping his left arm behind his back. The final 50 metres approached and Dan dropped both arms and just went for it—pure speed.

Dan won the Olympic gold and set a new world record, *because he changed his pattern*. Recognising that he owed his gold medal to his decision to change his pre-race routine, Dan later wrote about it in his book, Full Circle[9].

If you keep on doing things the same old way, you will keep getting the same results. If you aren't living the life you want, then change the way you think and the way you manage money.

Change your mind-set and your habits

How do you think of money? Is money fun, something that can provide you with all that you want, that can bring comfort, joy and pleasure into your life? Or is money something that you hate to think about, constantly talk about, a drudge, a burden, a weight on your mind, a source of anxiety?

Most people think that if they only had more money all of their problems would be over. But when you stop and think about this, it seems quite incongruous—why would you want more of something you hate, or find a burden? More money brings with it more responsibilities and, for many people, more anxieties. I can't tell you how many people I have advised who have come into money unexpectedly and found it incredibly stressful. Many of them have said, 'It was so much easier when I had no money. You think it's going to be wonderful, but there are so many choices'.

Prosperity does not come from the amount of money that you make, *it comes from what you do with what you have*. I have seen pensioners with fewer money worries and more freedom to do as they wish than some people who earn six-figure incomes. The fact that you are reading this book says that you want more money in your life, so change the way you feel about money. Think of money as a commodity that brings pleasure, ease and comfort. Not only will you enjoy thinking about how to spend money but you will understand how important good management of money is.

Change the way you talk about money. Stop limiting what you can have by talking like everyone else. If you are not sure what I mean, just observe for one day what people around you say about money. You'll be shocked how often people mention money in their daily conversation and how they use the lack of it to limit their choices. Are you one of those people who is always talking about money? Would you still do it if you knew you could have everything you want?

The question to ask yourself is, 'Do my behaviour and habits bring me the results that I want?' If you answer 'Yes', then leave them alone, but if you answer 'No' then change your behaviour and habits (your patterns). You can look at the way that you have managed money in the past and decide that reassessing your budget is a challenge rather than a chore. How can you still enjoy the same quality of life and have money left over? How can you better understand investments and taxation, so that you can maximise your returns?

Now, most people who think they want more (but really don't, because then they would have to think about it), hand their money over to investment advisers and say, 'Tell me what to do and I'll do it'. A lot of investment advisers just love this sort of client, because that's how they (the advisers) get wealthy. Believe me, there is no shortage of clients who don't want to take responsibility.

Choose positive habits

Some people have never had an experience of managing money efficiently. Their family history established a pattern of managing from week to week. They have carried on a pattern of spending and managing money that makes life difficult for them, because they have not done it any other way.

Change the way you have always done things. Think up strategies that you can put in place when you feel tempted to lapse back into bad habits. For instance, if you go to the automatic teller two or three times a week to withdraw money as you need it, STOP DOING IT. Work out how much you need for the week, withdraw once a week, place the money in a jar and give yourself a daily allowance. If you spend more than your daily allowance, try to make do until next week.

Have a short-term, extremely pleasurable goal that you save for NOW. You may want a home of your own, but that may be too daunting a goal unless you have a history of succeeding at financial goals. Choose something you can achieve in the short term, that makes you feel good (but you must save the money first), like a weekend away at a luxury resort. That may seem to be sheer extravagance and do nothing to advance your main goal of obtaining a home of your own. Actually, it will do more to help you achieve your goal than just saving relentlessly. In your subconscious each success creates a history (a memory) of success. As you achieve more and more goals, you will find that you manage money differently, because you begin to acknowledge that you really can achieve larger goals.

I used to spend everything I earned and always lived week to week. It was only when I started achieving goals that I was able to change my habits. I am no longer daunted by goals that appear way out of reach because I have a history of success. If I say to friends, 'This is what I want to do, but I have no idea how I will get the money to pay for it', they always say, 'Well that's not a problem, you always find it'. I always do.

If you hate paying bills, pay your bills with your credit card; you can do this by phone with most of them. Once a month you write out one cheque to the credit card company. This saves paper, stamps and bank charges and it can change paying bills from a painful experience to one that is easy. If you spend all your money on clothes, STOP GOING TO THE SHOPS. Find some other pleasurable activity to do instead. At one time I had a problem with credit cards because I was always in the shops. I stopped shopping and only went to the shops when I needed something, and I only carried my credit card when I knew in advance what I was purchasing. For quite some time I gave up using credit cards altogether. I no longer have that problem and can now carry my credit cards all the time. My values have changed and I no longer need the instant gratification that comes from shopping.

When my magazine closed down and I made the decision to

take time off, I decided it was a good time to reassess my spending. The question foremost in my mind was how I could reduce my living costs without reducing my lifestyle. I managed to cut spending by $100 a week. To achieve this, one of the things that I used regularly was a barter club; I made other changes as well. $100 week is not a fortune, but it adds up to $5,200 a year. That may not seem like a huge amount but, if it was invested over 20 years at 10 per cent, it would grow to $328,000. Now imagine if you could increase your savings even more—what choices would that give you?

If you want to create habits that support you in achieving your goals, then *interrupt the old patterns* and find a substitute behaviour. I believe in miracles, I believe that we attract opportunities, but when we work only with mind powers, it's a way of opting out of taking responsibility for ourselves. It's expecting the universe to give us what we won't give ourselves—and that doesn't make sense.

Associate pain with your old habits

Susan had two defaults on her credit record (a default can be recorded when you are behind on your payments). She knew she was able to pay her bills and wasn't really concerned about the defaults until she applied for a home loan. She was turned down for finance, for something that she really wanted, because of her past history.

She said to me, 'I never realised that I was being irresponsible, I always knew that I was going to pay. When I realised that this record might stop me from getting my own home I changed immediately'. Susan paid out both accounts and found a bank that would lend her the money, after some explanations. She learned a valuable lesson; she now makes a point of paying all accounts on, or before, the due date.

CHANGING YOUR PERSONAL HISTORY

Our memories, whether we like it or not, affect our present and our future. When an unpleasant (or painful) emotion occurs, we either deal with it or repress it. Modern-day culture encourages us to repress our emotions. We frown upon people who are 'too emotional'. Bob Hawke, when Prime Minister, cried on national television while talking about his daughter's drug addiction and made headlines all around the world. However, when we don't deal with our emotions, they still carry an emotional charge that can influence our decisions and create illness.

During one seminar, I learnt that dyslexia results from stress. Gordon Stokes and Daniel Whiteside, authors of *One Brain*[10] wrote, 'Dyslexia results from emotional stress at the time of learning, a stress so intense that the individual programs in a blind spot to a given learning skill due to fear, fear of pain, or pain itself'. My kinesiologist, working with one brain techniques, has actually assisted people to cure their dyslexia.

Many people have a blind spot when it comes to money. When I gave investment or practical advice on money to clients I saw many of them literally 'switch off' the moment I would start to explain something to them. If I changed the subject and started talking about their family, I would regain their attention.

In order to change the pattern, you need to change the emotional charge around the memory. One very simple technique is to scramble the sensations we link to a particular memory. Imagine you have had a bad day, everything went wrong and everybody took their anger out on you. You could replay the events in your mind only this time see the humour in it. Make up funny experiences if need be. When you talk about the incident to your family and friends, recall the humour. Next time you remember it, you'll have changed the memory from a painful one to a funny one.

Another simple way to release stress I learnt from my kinesiologist. Lightly hold the forehead with the palm of one hand, and the back of the head (just above the neck) with the palm of the other hand. You may find it less tiring on the arms if you lie down. Think about the problem. After a while the brain will either find a solution to the problem or wander off. This demonstrates that the issue has been dealt with.

Pam Mountfield, a specialised kinesiologist practicing in Sydney says, 'This procedure works through the use of acupressure. When there is light pressure on the forehead, the brain increases blood flow to that area. This part of the brain, the frontal lobe, has the function of present and future thinking, or new choices. The hand on the back of the head is connecting to the back brain, which is where our past thinking occurs. By holding both the front and the back lightly, you are allowing the brain to choose new options, instead of resorting to past unsuccessful patterns'.

TIME LINE THERAPY™

Another technique I have found helpful is Time Line Therapy™. This is a fairly simple technique that involves going back in your mind to a time in the past and defusing that memory. Often experiences that run our lives took place when we were only young and didn't have the resources we have today. We can take the resources we have now (or create resources if you need to), and mentally travel back to our past so that we look down on the event, and change the memory.

The advantage that Time Line Therapy™, has over other techniques is that if you go back in your mind to the very first instance and clear that memory, all of the later experiences automatically clear. Occasionally, this doesn't happen, so you may need to continue clearing memories until you feel that they have all been dealt with.

Tad James, the creator of Time Line Therapy™, once said, 'I'm not into pain. I believe we can overcome problems without having to do years of therapy. I discovered that we can release negative emotions using Time Line Therapy™ whilst talking to a student. She said, "I have all this anger about an event in the past". But when she went back to the time before the event the anger was gone. It didn't make sense. So it was a couple more years before I realised that you could take out all of the anger from a person's past'.

Tad's work is being used to assist people with medical problems. Tad tells a story of a Dr Hamer whose son, aged eighteen, was shot and killed. A few years later, Dr Hamer developed testicular cancer, was operated on, and survived. Afterwards, he wondered whether or not severe emotional trauma, such as he had suffered upon the violent death of his son, precedes all cancer. Dr Hamer research over 10,000 cases of people with cancer.

Tad James related what happened, 'Dr Hamer flatly states that all cancer starts with a severe psychological conflict that throws you into shock. He says, "You isolate yourself, and do not share your emotions with others. You are upset and you're obsessed about the conflict. This conflict changes your life completely—you will never be the same". This is a description of a significant emotional experience, or SEE. This type of SEE, according to Hamer, usually occurs on the average of one to three years prior to the onset of the first symptoms of cancer.

'When the SEE occurs, the emotions associated with the SEE are trapped in a certain spot in the brain and, according to Hamer, a "short circuit" occurs. In his work, Hamer has connected the spot in the brain with the related tumour in the body, and the likely type of trauma which caused it. Hamer says the answer is to heal the brain'.

Chapter 6 – Changing Patterns

A number of people have used Time Line Therapy™ to change their personal history, with startling results. Some cancer sufferers claim that when they altered their personal history, their cancer started shrinking and eventually disappeared. Time Line is a simple technique but you may need help from an accredited therapist, or complete a course on it if you have not done it before. I'll give you an example of how I used it to clear my fear of humiliation.

If you remember, my strongest 'moving away' from my personal values was caused by fear of humiliation. In order to achieve my goals, I needed to remove the emotional charge from past memories. I did this by asking myself the question, 'When was the first humiliating experience I remember?' I took the first age that came to mind. I relaxed, closed my eyes, and imagined rising above my body and travelling along my time line until 15 minutes prior to this first occurrence. I still felt stress, so I knew that this was not the first time it had happened, so I travelled back through time to an early age.

I arrived at a time when humiliation was not an issue. I imagined I was in a position overhead 15 minutes before the event took place. I asked myself what lesson could be learnt from that experience and when I discovered what the lesson was, I cut an imaginary line, that was my emotional attachment to that memory, and released the stress. As I travelled back through time to my present, I checked memories of past experiences that were humiliating to see if I still felt stress. I felt none, so the exercise was complete.

Now, some of you reading this are going to think this is really wacky, but this method is now being used by the Department of Medicine at The University of Calgary in Canada, in one of its oncology treatment classes for medical students. A Michigan college also teaches it to its psychology students, Dr Deepak

Chopra's medical institute uses the technique, and other enlightened medical centres are following suit.

FORGIVENESS

Forgiveness is a vital part of the process of change. You cannot change a memory and still hold on to anger against another person. It's not always easy to forgive, but ask yourself, 'Who is being hurt by my anger?' You'll find the only person being hurt is yourself.

Some people confuse forgiveness with condoning a person's behaviour—you can forgive a person without approving of their ethics.

SECONDARY GAIN

Once you have worked at eliminating the power of past memories, there may be one more step to take. There is often a secondary gain for staying in a situation (I refer to this in *Financially Free* as pay-offs). For instance, you may want more money and financial freedom, but know this will jeopardise your marriage. You may want fame and fortune but don't want to leave your old friends behind. Having money problems may be your way of gaining attention, or stop you taking responsibility for yourself. The list of possibilities goes on and on.

If you do feel that there is a benefit from having these problems, ask yourself how you can fulfil this need without having to give up your goal. You may be able to find other strategies that will give you the same benefit without sabotaging your goals. You have every right to stay exactly as you are right now, but be aware of the consequences of your choices—the same behaviour will bring the same results. You can control your memories, or your memories can control you.

SUMMARY

Change your mind-set and your habits.

Decide on substitute behaviour in advance so that you aren't tempted to fall back on old habits. If you fall back into old patterns do something immediately to interrupt the pattern.

Develop positive new habits that support your goals. Look for different ways to achieve goals.

Experiment with techniques until you find the one that works best for you to eliminate the power of old memories.

NOTES

CHAPTER SEVEN

LIFE IS WHAT YOU MAKE IT

It's not what happens to you. It's what you do about it.

W Mitchell

*The past is gone,
and clinging to
events,
people,
or expectations
only hinders
your success
today.*

One phrase I remember hearing Denis Waitley say at a seminar has stayed with me for years. He said, 'What you thought yesterday, has created your world today. What you think today, creates your world tomorrow'. What type of tomorrow are you creating?

A woman rang me one day needing an appointment urgently. I agreed to see her the next day. It turned out that she had debts that she couldn't pay and one creditor was threatening to garnishee her wages. She worked for a company that set very high standards: employees were expected to manage their affairs and she knew having unmanageable debts would be frowned on. She said she would do anything to avoid the humiliation and the possibility of losing her job. There were some practical steps that this woman could take and I told her what she could do, but I was more concerned as to why she created this situation in the first place, as it was a recurring pattern in her life.

When I asked what her values were she said, 'What other people think and appearances'. When I pushed for a few more she added in family and friends. That was it. I then asked what emotion she would do anything to avoid facing, and she said, not surprisingly, 'humiliation and rejection'. Trying to find out what was behind her decisions, I asked, 'What has to happen in order for you to feel prosperous?' and she answered, 'Get out of this mess'. Next, I asked her to presume the problem had been dealt with, and asked the same question. She had no idea. Every decision, every action this woman took was to impress others—she had no other goals.

When you lurch from one crisis to another and, believe me, some people do, you will continue to get more of the same. Your thoughts today create your tomorrow.

We may have no control over the past, but we can change how we perceive it. We always have control over our present and our future. You can choose to be happy with what you have, while still working on creating more, or you can be miserable.

Ask yourself these questions: 'What has to happen in order for me to experience abundance?', 'Do I have to have a certain level of income?', 'A certain standard of living?', 'Do I have to own property and investments?' and 'Be debt-free?'

Our expectations are the rules we apply in order to be happy or fulfilled. Just like beliefs, our values and rules are generally not a conscious choice—they are the result of our conditioning. Think back to the things that you were told you should do, or must do. The shoulds and musts in your life make up the rules that you live by. These rules will also influence all of your decisions.

Some people have rules that they must save, be responsible with money, and provide for their future. They may also have rules that you cannot take risks, or do anything that would jeopardise financial security. Others, like the woman I mentioned earlier in this chapter had no such rules. Her rules dictated that it was important to be liked, that it was important to live in a good suburb and drive a nice car, regardless of the consequences. Her rules said that it was okay to get in a mess, but not okay to be found out.

It's not a matter of whether your rules are right or wrong. The question is do your rules empower you? Do they make it easy for you to achieve your goals?

If you are unsure of what your rules are, then monitor your self-talk. Every time you hear yourself say 'I should', or 'I must' you have discovered another rule. Barbara Tebo, whose story I told in Chapter Four said, 'If we have no shoulds, we have no stress'.

Your perceptions are governed by your rules

Most people have heard the expression about half a cup of coffee. Whether you see the cup as half-full, or half-empty depends on your perception of life. This perception flows from the rules that you live by, which dictate whether you will have a pleasurable response or a painful response.

If your rules dictate that you should own a home by a certain age and you don't, then you are going to feel stress. If your rules dictate that a man should support a woman then, if you are a woman, you will probably find ways to spend all of your money waiting for Mr Right to come along. If you are a man with the same rules, however, you may not be comfortable with you wife working. If she does, you will probably encourage her to keep her own money while you pay all the bills. If your rules dictate that you have to dress a certain way, drive a certain car (usually in order to be noticed), then you'll most likely have debt problems. Remember the couple I mentioned earlier who wanted to achieve all of their major financial goals (house renovation, new car, holiday, new career) before their baby was born? The man probably had some rules about providing financial stability, or a certain lifestyle, before having children.

Our rules not only govern our choices but they also influence how we will react when life doesn't go the way we planned.

It's not what happens to you, it's what you do about it!

A quite exceptional man called Mitchell (he prefers to be called this), wrote a wonderful book two years ago entitled *The Man who would not be Defeated*[11]. In the introduction, he wrote, 'I have a great life. You can have a great life too'. When you read of some of the events of Mitchell's life, you will realise what a remarkable person he is to be able to make such a statement.

One morning in July 1971, at 28 years of age, Mitchell was riding high. He had a job that he loved, a good relationship, and he had just fulfilled a lifelong dream—to fly solo in an aeroplane. The day before, Mitchell had picked up his new motorcycle. It was not just any motorcycle, 'It was a Honda 750, the biggest, snazziest, meanest cycle on the market. I adored it', he said.

Mitchell was driving his new motorcycle up a street in San Francisco when a truck turned, cutting him off. He hit the truck in the side—and went down, breaking his elbow and pelvis. The lid of his petrol tank popped open, and petrol came gushing out and ignited. In a split second a fireball three metres high and more than a metre wide had engulfed him. The hospital was not optimistic about his survival—there were burns to over 65 per cent of his body. Mitchell went into a coma and did not come out of it for two weeks. His eyelids were sewn shut to keep them moist and he had a tracheotomy tube inserted into his throat to help him breathe.

Mitchell said later that being a burns patient is something you can't imagine: something terribly painful is being done to you virtually every hour of the day. He had 16 skin grafts in four months and the surgeons had to cut off his fingers—all that remained on each hand were a couple of stumps just over one centimetre long. When they told Mitchell they could not save his fingers, he said, 'Wow, this is going to destroy my pool game'.

Looking back on this response, Mitchell said, 'Well, what could I say? "I'm gonna strangle you!" The guy had done the best he could. Once I had fingers, now I didn't. Whatever meaning this had, would be the meaning I gave it. I could see it as a catastrophe, or as a challenge. I chose the latter'.

Mitchell started putting his life back together and almost immediately started flying again. He was awarded a settlement from the insurance company but after lawyers' fees, he received only $500,000. However, he started investing in businesses and in property and soon became a millionaire.

Determined to pick up the threads of his life Mitchell bought his own plane, and qualified to fly again in spite of his hands, within five years he had accomplished a lot. One day, he took off from the airport with a full load, but when they were only at 30 metres he realised that the plane was very sluggish. They still had runway left. Mitchell decided to land. The plane stalled in the air and dropped hard onto the runway.

Mitchell screamed to his passengers to get out—visions of another explosion raced through his mind. As he tried to break free from his seat, he found he could not move his legs. Later, in hospital, he was told he was paralysed, and would remain a paraplegic for the rest of his life.

Mitchell later said that at first he wondered, 'Why me?' After a recovery period, he got on with his life again—entering politics, running his businesses and fighting for causes he believed in. Tony Robbins asked Mitchell to speak at one of his seminars and a whole new career opened up. He now travels the world, regularly inspiring and motivating others.

Mitchell now says, 'My business is my pleasure. Some people say "Get realistic, how can I enjoy changing tyres?" I ask them, "What is your purpose? What are you here for?" My scars are visible, but there are more people with scars on the inside. People who live in mental wheelchairs. Some people think— why me, why doesn't the prime minister make things better, why is everyone out to get me? I talk to groups and companies and I say, "Have you had a bad day? Can you have a bad half-day? Is it possible it could be a bad hour?" You could decide there's a lot of great things to think about. You could think about what is right. What you can do. What you can change to make your day better'.

Mitchell lives by the rule that you make the most of your life, no matter what. He has achieved goals that ordinary people only dream about. He has homes in Santa Barbara and Hawaii, is a multi-millionaire with diverse business interests, and travels the world regularly, in spite of his physical handicaps.

When I interviewed him we were sitting in the coffee shop of the luxury hotel where he was staying, overlooking Sydney Harbour. I noticed how many people stopped to chat—people accept Mitchell's handicaps because he does. Mitchell has severe scarring, has stumps for fingers and is confined to a wheelchair, but you would never think of treating, or even thinking of, Mitchell as handicapped. You don't feel sympathy for Mitchell, you feel admiration.

Are you waiting for your life to be perfect so you can be happy? Do you jeopardise your future success by having to live up to appearances? Are the goals you set really the ones that you want? Will they fulfil you?

You always have a choice: you can choose to enjoy each day, you can choose new goals if the old ones create too much pressure on you, you can choose how you will respond to any situation. You can look for the lesson and the good in everything—no matter what happens to you.

Happiness is a choice

I once believed that if I only found the right man, preferably an ambitious one, I would be happy. I eventually met a man who seemed to fit my criteria and for a time, I believed that I was in love. I started out working for him, then we became business partners. When he started another business, I became a director of that business as well. We were a good team—our enterprises were making good profits and life looked good.

Ever since my son Robbie had been born five years earlier, I had been setting goals and working on creating a success consciousness. I listened to Denis Waitley's 'The Psychology of Winning' tapes until they fell apart; they had a tremendous influence on my life. One night I looked around me, at my two beautiful children, and thought, 'If I never have any more than this, that's okay'. I had all that mattered to me.

A few days later, my children and I attended the birthday party of a friend's daughter—Valerie's daughter, Sara, would be six. I felt uncomfortable all day and wanted to ring and cancel, but logic and reason prevailed. However, I did take particular care watching my son Robbie, aged five, in the pool. The party ended, the children went home. Robbie and the birthday girl Sara went off to play with her presents. I relaxed and went into Valerie's bedroom to look at her new clothes.

Shortly afterwards there was a hurried knock on the door. A woman cried, 'A child has fallen off the balcony!' We were five storeys high. At first we thought the child was Sara, but I knew in my heart it was Robbie. He was a demon for climbing and escaping.

It seemed like an eternity before the lift arrived. I prayed out loud in front of a lift full of strangers, who were giving me weird looks. Finally we reached the ground. Robbie was lying on the concrete driveway. Amazingly unmarked except for a gaping hole where his nose had been. He was still alive. I remember thinking, 'plastic surgeons can do wonders these days'. He'll be alright. Not for one moment did I doubt he would survive.

Acting purely on instinct, I placed my hands gently on him and said, 'I want you to live, but if you want to go it's okay'. A few minutes later he died.

It would be a lie to say the months that followed were easy. The pain was so intense that at times I didn't think I would make it through the day. I would cling to the minute. Through all the ups and downs of my life, my children were, and are, my greatest love. I doubt there is any greater pain than losing one's child.

A month after Robbie died, my business partner and I split up. I was suddenly without an income, a place to go each day, everything that was familiar. My eldest daughter, Lisa, was just starting high school. I regret that I was of no help to her whatsoever.

Some people say you never get over such a loss, but you learn to live with it. I believe that you can get over it if you don't resist it. By that, I mean just letting the experience be—feel the pain, the guilt, the depths of despair whatever emotions arise. Eventually they will pass. Nothing can minimise the pain. I can remember thinking that if I allowed myself to feel all the pain, I would shatter into pieces. Surprisingly, I didn't.

In the midst of all that pain there was a positive side. I experienced the most exquisite feeling of love that I have never felt before or since. The day after Robbie died, I went for a walk about 5 a.m. As the sun rose, I felt Robbie's presence on one side of me, and an unknown presence on the other side. I felt totally loved and supported. This experience eliminated any fears of death I may have had.

Although I grew up in a religious family, my spiritual awakening began with Robbie's death. I feel so grateful to have been blessed with this child for five wonderful years. I grew so much as a person by knowing him, through his life and his death.

I made a conscious decision that my son would not die in vain. The only power I had was to change myself and I decided that my life would mean something. It took a few years before I began working on my life's purpose: I had some grieving to do. But I believe that I was led into work that helped others; through my books, my courses and my newsletter, I hope that I can use what I have learnt to make life richer for others.

If I had not had so much positive reinforcement from the books I'd read, the tapes I'd played and the seminars that I'd attended for years beforehand, I doubt I would have had the knowledge or resources to make such a choice. It changed my life dramatically. Prior to this I expected 'other people' to make me happy, but all that work on myself paid off when I needed it most.

Every day, I hear people complaining about their situation, particularly their lack of money, jobs and opportunities. Yet, at the same time, all of these people have a roof over their heads and most of them have regular incomes. We live in one of the most beautiful parts of the world. We have freedom, we have choices, yet the majority of people focus on what they don't have.

You have a choice. No-one, let me repeat no-one can tell you how to react to any situation. You can choose to be happy no matter what happens to you; you can choose to be prosperous even though, right now your circumstances may not look positive. You can program yourself to look for the good in every situation, after a while you don't consciously think of it, and it becomes automatic.

When you do what you love, and take responsibility for yourself and your actions, abundance follows. The same applies to relationships. Many women, particularly, deny themselves the lives they want because they believe it is a man's place to provide for them. I once had that belief, but I know that the only person who can fulfil my dreams is me. I no longer need a man in my life to be happy. Are the rules that you live by hindering you, or helping you?

YOU CAN CHANGE YOUR RULES

Tony Robbins once told the story of a man who attended one of his seminars. By just about anyone's standards, this man was a success. When Tony asked him what had to happen in order for him to feel successful, he replied that he had to earn $3 million a year in straight salary. He was already earning $3.5 million a year, but that was made up of a salary of only $1.5 million plus bonuses. He also had to have eight per cent body fat, in order to feel successful—he had nine per cent—and he had to never get frustrated with his kids. I doubt, with this set of rules, whether this man could ever be happy.

At the same seminar was a man who had so much energy he seemed to be bouncing off the walls. Tony asked, 'Are you successful?' The man beamed as he said, 'Absolutely!' when Tony asked him what he needed to have happen in order for him to feel successful, he replied, 'Every day above ground is a great day!'[8]

It would be nice to go through life with no rules, but I doubt if we would have the motivation to achieve much. Rules are not bad things but choose rules that make it easy for you to feel good about yourself.

You can change your rules to support your values. For instance, I value self-expression; I need a rule to support that. If I decide that everyone has to love my books and courses, I'm setting myself up to be hurt. My new rule is that not everyone is going to like what I say, and that's okay. Now, if no-one read my books or purchased my home-study program then I would know that I was not communicating effectively, I would have to do something.

Another rule I live by is that I will not accept less than what I really want. It is that rule that has given me the persistence and courage to go on, to learn more, to experiment, change and succeed.

Do you expect other to live by your rules?

As well as placing expectations (rules) upon ourselves, we place them on others, too. We can create unnecessary stress by expecting people to live up to our expectations.

Money is often a source of conflict in relationships, usually because one person doesn't live according to the rules or values of the other. For example, one person may believe that buying flowers makes them feel prosperous, while the other may think it's an extravagance. You need to sit down with your partner and clearly communicate what your rules are about money. Define what you consider necessary and what you consider extravagant. Listen to what your partner has to say, then work at formulating new rules that will meet both your needs.

Communicate your rules

Communicate your rules, not only to your partner, but also to your employees, your children and your friends. I have a friend who describes herself as a 'black and white' person—a thing is either right or wrong. I'm much more shades of 'grey'. My rules aren't as rigid as hers, and I don't agree with everything that she says, nor she with me. We've known each other for 32 years and we've both learnt a lot in that time; I've come to accept her as she is and she accepts me, and we respect each other's right to have different opinions.

I have a cousin, though, who hasn't talked to me for years, and I assume I must have broken one of her rules. As children, we always got on well but as Jenny is seven years younger than me, we were at different life stages. However, as an adult, I moved to a house not far from her, and as we have children of a similar age, we became very good friends, talking on the phone a few times a week and usually seeing each other once if not more often each week. But, towards the end of our friendship, I noticed she was not as friendly and was becoming more irritable. I put it down to it being the end of the year, thinking she probably needed a holiday. Then one day on the phone she exploded, and said she was fed up with me. When I asked what the problem was, she said, 'Well, you should know. If you don't know, that only makes it worse'.

Jenny has not talked to me since. She did not return my phone calls, or respond to my notes to have coffee and talk, and now, five years later I have no idea what I did, but obviously I broke one of her cardinal rules. You can't expect others to live by your rules, if you don't tell them what they are.

SUMMARY

Your 'musts' and 'shoulds' are the rules you live by.

If your rules don't support you, change them.

Look for the lesson, and the gift, in every painful situation.

We all have a choice—we can triumph over adversity, or we can become victims.

Set up your rules to support your goals, and don't have too many rules.

Communicate your rules to others, but better still, don't expect other people to live up to your expectations.

NOTES

CHAPTER EIGHT

TUNING INTO ABUNDANCE

*Abundance flows
when we love
what we are doing.*

Wayne Dyer

*Consciously
choose
thoughts
that will make
your life
the way
you
want it to be.*

Chapter 8 – Tuning Into Abundance

I once read a fascinating story in Reader's Digest[17]. Thom and his wife, Rita, were struggling to put out a small weekly newspaper in Guthrie, Oklahoma. Thom did the writing and Lisa sold the ads. Often they would work past midnight.

One morning, they crawled out of bed after just a few hours' sleep. Thom had cereal and a large soft drink for breakfast and set off to the printers saying, as he left the house, that he was so tired he shouldn't be driving. Lisa organised the children for school, equally as tired, but then she set about ringing creditors and asking for an extension of time to pay their bills.

The large soft drink had its effect and Thom realised he would never make it to the city, so he pulled over at a rest stop on the highway just a few kilometres from home.

As Thom stepped from the car, he heard the public phone at the rest stop ring. He looked around and since he was the only person there, he picked up the receiver. Silence was followed by a shriek. It was Lisa. She asked what Thom was doing at the electricity company. Thom asked what she was doing ringing a public phone at a rest stop. They stayed on the phone and began talking, really talking without interruptions. That conversation was to change their lives. They both wondered how they had become so devoted to their work that they could leave their children with a stranger to put them to bed. How could they have breakfast together and be too tired to say good morning?

That conversation led them to reassess their priorities. Later, they sold the business and rearranged their lives. Was the wrong phone number that Lisa dialed just a coincidence? Thom doesn't believe so. He knows more than anything else that morning, they needed to hear each other's voices.

I don't believe in coincidences. We can all learn to draw into our lives the people, opportunities, skills that we need in order to achieve our desires.

THE LAW OF ATTRACTION

The universe is pure energy. For years, I read and taught about the 'law of attraction', not understanding how it worked. Now science is providing the answers. There is a new science called biophysics which investigates the natural energy field around the body and how it works. This is not really a new discovery, since ancient civilisations and indigenous people have always had this knowledge.

We accept such things as radio, TV, communications satellites, microwaves and computers as everyday things. They all work by transmitting energy over the airwaves, so it shouldn't be too hard to accept that our bodies transmit and receive energy in much the same way. Our bodies act as two-way radios[12], tuned to transmit and receive electromagnetic energy. Every part of us, every cell, every organ, every gland, every thought sends and receives information. Different parts of the body transmit and receive at different frequencies (much like a radio station). The eyes receive frequencies between 390 and 780 trillion cycles per second, while the ears receive frequencies between 20 and 20,000 cycles per second.

Our thoughts vibrate at different frequencies for different emotions. For instance, if fear rules your decisions, you will be tuned into that particular frequency, and you will, in turn, attract into your life others who are also fearful. We attract or repel opportunities depending on the frequency we are tuned in to; in other words when we feel optimistic we attract opportunities, when we feel fearful, we repel them. It doesn't matter how talented you are, or how hard you work.

At one time, I used to have a massage every month and the woman I went to was excellent at her job, but she never had enough clients and was always worrying about money. There were many times when I would go to make an appointment at the end of the massage, and would suddenly change my mind. Sometimes, I would ring up with the intention of making an appointment, and then change my mind—the only explanation I could give was that it didn't feel right. I believe that this woman was at times 'tuned-in' to a different frequency to me.

In 1966[13], an American expert on polygraph examination, the lie detector test, decided to hook up his galvanometer to one of the plants in the office, a philodrendron. To see if he could get a reaction, he dunked the leaves of the plant in hot coffee. There was no reaction, but when he burned a leaf with a match, the galvanometer went wild. He tested hundreds of other plants and every test confirmed that plants have cognitive powers.

During one experiment, a researcher destroyed one of two plants. Using the galvanometer as a communication tool, the remaining plant was able to identify, from six suspects, who was responsible. If a plant can read a person's thoughts, surely we can learn to tune in as well.

One woman told the story of her family's bird, who absolutely adored the man of the house. Her husband was in business and worked irregular hours, arriving home at different times each day, but she always knew when he was nearby because the bird would started screeching and become excited about 10 minutes prior to his master's arrival. The bird was 'tuned-in' to his owner's energy field.

As we understand energy levels more, we get a clearer understanding of why one person succeeds whereas another fails. My local garage changed hands recently. Previously it was just an ordinary garage but I went there because the attendant served you. Then the sign went up, 'Under New Management'. I can't say I thought much about it until I saw the queues.

The new owner was a very bright, cheery man, despite being

run off his feet who, for no apparent reason, attracted a very large clientele. No matter what time of day, or day of the week I go, there is always a queue. Everything about the garage remains unchanged—their prices are the same and the service is the same (except for the cheery attitude). I've also noticed that when the owner is not there, the queues get smaller. The increased patronage can only be explained by the different owners—different thoughts create different realities.

You not only tune into a frequency, you can tune others out. That is how you block opportunities in your life. I told the story earlier of how I created the opportunity to set up a women's investment advisory service; that opportunity could have been available to me a lot sooner.

At the time, I was working as office manager for a funds management company. Impressive title, but I had little to do. My main task was to see that the office functioned smoothly; as I'm very efficient, it did. So my day would consist of checking the supplies of wine and spirits, ordering stationery and doing other mundane tasks. In order to have something to do, I'd fill in for the receptionist at lunchtime or write up books for the accountant. Some of the other managers became aware that I had time to spare, so any extra collating came to me. After working for nearly 20 years, I didn't relish doing the office junior's job. I was frustrated and even though I worked at keeping my focus on what I wanted (my wonderful new job), a lot of my thoughts were negative.

When the call finally came asking if I was interested in another position I discovered that John had been trying to call me for six months, but because I was so frustrated, I had actually emitted energy that blocked this opportunity coming to me.

Our bodies act as aerials, sending and receiving signals. Each person's aerial is unique because of their DNA, their genetic material, and the frequencies that they tune into, are unique. This goes a long way towards explaining clairvoyant and psychic activity. Now, I am not clairvoyant and I believe that very few who make their living telling fortunes are genuine. However, I have always been able to pick up other people's thoughts. I am always ringing people just when they are thinking about me.

My son went missing when he was two years old—he was a real houdini. After looking for him in all the obvious places, and driving around for two hours, along with the police and neighbours, I suddenly had a clear picture in my mind of someone holding him in their arms by the side of the road, a couple of blocks from our house. As I drove over the hill there they were, exactly as I had seen them in my mind. It wasn't just coincidence, as this has happened to me many times.

I once had a very close relationship with a man. I knew things about him long before he would tell me—you can imagine what problems that created! When our relationship ended, he moved interstate. I did not see or hear of him for years, nor mix with any of his friends. One day, I was preparing dinner and the thought popped into my head, 'He's living back in Sydney'. Out of curiosity I made a phone call and discovered that he had moved back just days before.

TUNING IN

In the past, these things 'just happened'. I had no idea how they happened, and certainly had no control over them. As I have begun to understand how electromagnetic vibrations work, I can now tune in when I need information rather than just letting things happen.

If you have felt optimistic as you have read this book you have probably increased your level of vibrations. That is why we feel so good when we go to a motivational seminar or a concert—we get swept along by the group energy. It doesn't last long though; once we return to our everyday life, we return to normal. If, however, you have worked out your goals, values and needs as you've gone along, you will already have discovered a lot about yourself and what has influenced your past decisions. As you have made changes, you will have altered the level of vibrations around you. You may even have started listening to your instincts and acting upon them. Your instincts, or intuition, are your best resource for answers to decisions you need to make.

One morning, Pam Mountfield, the kinesiologist referred to in Chapter Six, was driving to her naturopathic clinic. She was 20 metres away from a set of traffic lights when they turned yellow and she could easily have gone through them in time, but an inner voice yelled 'STOP', and she did, instantly. On the other side of the road, a young woman, around 25, started to cross the street. Suddenly, a truck laden with paper rolls, came around a blind corner. It was travelling too fast to stop.

The truck hit the girl on the pedestrian crossing, dragging her body under the heavy vehicle. Her body came out the other side and the truck stopped just a metre short of Pam's car. She was still 20 metres back from the crossing.

Later on, as the policeman took down the details of the accident from Pam, he said he couldn't understand why she had stopped her car so far back from the crossing. When she told him about her inner voice that had yelled 'STOP', he said that if she had stopped at the crossing she would probably be dead.

Pam said, 'I found out the following day that the young girl died of internal injuries. I found it hard to accept at first. I eventually accepted that it was her time. I thanked her for this incredible learning experience. I learnt I can be calm in a disaster, that I did do my best on that day. Most importantly, she helped me to become more trusting of my little voice. I am now constantly guided by this little voice which I believe comes from a higher realm. Some may say it's God, or gut feelings, or just plain old intuition. I don't need a name, I give thanks daily for its presence'.

How do you differentiate between intuition and plain old worry? There are no shortcuts, it takes practise. Some say intuition is a feeling, whereas worry is a little voice you hear. My intuition comes as both feelings and voices. Sometimes I hear a voice , a kind of internal dialogue, that tells me what to do. One day while I was working my little voice said, 'Check the time', so I looked at my watch. It was operating fine and I ignored the warning. I arrived at my daughter's school 20 minutes late because the time on my watch was wrong.

Nancy Rosanoff, author of *Intuition Workout* said, 'If (a thought) comes back to me three times, I do it. Intuitions are insistent and persistent. If it is important, you will not forget it. It will keep coming back to you. It will nag you...'[14]

Practise on little things, take note of the feeling and the outcome. It will take time to differentiate the two but you will soon know the difference.

In their book, *The Celestine Prophecy, an Experiential Guide*[13] James Redfield and Carol Adrienne said, 'Intellect-centred messages might:

- be based on scarcity, fear or guilt
- be based on protecting oneself
- be compelling, with no time to reflect
- be quick answers, and feel out of context with your flow
- be the first thing that comes to mind
- feel like a desperate need

Intuitive-centred messages are:

- loving and reassuring
- encouraging and positive
- not usually demanding immediate action
- rarely radical without smaller steps to initiate change'.

Obviously this applies to testing decisions. If you have an emergency such as Pam experienced whilst driving her car, you are going to get an urgent message and sometimes you have to act rather than waiting to check it out.

Another way to test your choices is to ask yourself a question. For instance, 'Should I buy this house?' How does your body respond? If it feels comfortable, you know you can go ahead. If your body feels uncomfortable with the answer, it's not right for you at this time.

THE POWER OF THOUGHT

Our thoughts create our reality, so take care what you dwell on. Dr Deepak Chopra tells a story of a fireman who came into the emergency room at the hospital where he worked complaining of sudden, sharp chest pains. The resident on call found nothing wrong and the fireman went away. However, he returned later with the same symptoms and was referred to Deepak. Despite extensive testing using the most sophisticated machinery, there was no evidence of anything being wrong with the man's heart.

The fireman returned on a regular basis with the same pains. Eventually Deepak recommended that he be retired for psychological reasons with a full disability pension. The fire department's medical examining board turned the application down on the grounds that there was no physical evidence. Two months later, the man showed up at the emergency room, the victim of a massive heart attack. Just before he died, he turned to Deepak and whispered, 'Now do you believe I have a heart condition?'

Another patient of Deepak's complained of severe abdominal pain. He admitted her for surgery believing it was gallstones, but the surgeons discovered malignant cancerous tumours in her liver and pockets of cancer in her abdominal cavity. The woman had only months to live and the surgeons could do nothing. The patient's daughter begged Deepak not to tell her mother, so Deepak told his patient that her problem was gallstones and they had been removed.

Eight months later, the woman returned to Deepak's office for a routine physical, which revealed no jaundice or signs of cancer. A year later, the woman returned again, even healthier and said, 'Doctor, I was so sure I had cancer two years ago that when it turned out to be just gallstones, I told myself I would never be sick another day in my life'[15]. Her cancer never returned.

Gifts can be developed

People often use excuses like 'I'm not gifted like you' or 'I don't have the talent'. A few exceptional people are born with gifts; the rest of us develop them with patience, perseverance and lots of practise.

Danielle Steele is one of the world's top selling romance novelists. She sells millions of her books and churns them out with amazing regularity. I read an article about her once that said she would think about a book for months, just let it develop in her mind, and then she would sit down and write it effortlessly.

That is exactly how I write.

I don't yet have the luxury of going away to an idyllic place and just writing. My number one joy in life is being a mother, so my work has to fit in with Laura's life. I write during school hours, and in between I have to answer letters and do messages. After school, I write while the children play and I'm often interrupted with requests for iceblocks, drinks or toys. I don't have time for writer's block, so I never have it. I couldn't always write. When I first had to reply to correspondence at work, it took me half a day to compose one letter. When I wrote my first book it took me three years. My second book took 24 days and this one will take about 30 days. There will be re-writes, editing and time spent discussing layout and style and so forth, but the actual writing of the manuscript will be about 30 days.

You develop gifts by learning how to use your mind. I made a sudden decision to start this book, so I didn't have the usual few months for it to develop itself. At first, it wasn't flowing. I told the same stories but they just didn't gel. So whenever the ideas stopped flowing, I would close my eyes and breathe in to the count of four, hold my breath for the count of four, release to the count of four, and pause to the count of four.

It takes me about two minutes to get centred again, but you can do it for any length of time that you want. I start back, ask for inspiration and the ideas flow again, or I'll go to my library and ask for the right book for the inspiration that I need. I open the book at random and there's my answer. I have more of a problem having to stop the creative flow to pick up the children from school (I take Laura and two friends), but it is my choice to be a full-time mum, so I put up with that inconvenience.

Everyone, no matter what age, no matter what level of intelligence can learn to tap into this most valuable resource.

Sandy MacGregor used his valuable resources to change feelings of grief, hurt and anger to acceptance, love and forgiveness.

TRAGEDY LED TO HELPING OTHERS

Sandy MacGregor first became interested in meditation and mind control when his eldest son, Andrew, used it to control asthma attacks. Sandy took Andrew to an Indian doctor who specialised in relaxation techniques, and soon Andrew was able to control his attacks. Andrew later injured his leg in an accident, breaking it in two places, and he used the same techniques to tolerate excruciating levels of pain and make a complete recovery.

Sandy asked Andrew to teach him the techniques but, after a year with no results, Sandy said, 'It works for you but not for me'. However, Sandy decided to give it another go and went back to the doctor. His goal was to lose weight. He meditated 20 minutes at a time, three times a day and nothing happened for six weeks. During the seventh week, he lost one kilo, then went on to lose 22 kilos in six months—without dieting or exercise. He was converted.

At 3 a.m. one morning, Sandy was woken by four policemen hammering at his door. His first thought was that something had happened to one of his teenage daughters. The police informed him that all three girls—the twins, Jenny and Kirsty, aged nineteen, and Lexi, aged sixteen—had been murdered, along with a friend. Richard Maddrell, the murderer, had gone out with one of the girls and refused to accept that the relationship had ended. At the time of the murder, Maddrell had been diagnosed as a paranoid schizophrenic, but had refused medication. On that fateful night, Maddrell had watched an American politician shoot himself on television in front of millions. Perhaps that influenced him in some way, because he took his gun to the girl's home (they lived with Sandy's first wife), and shot them. In court, Maddrell was found not guilty on the grounds of mental illness. He is now in a ward for the criminally insane in one of Sydney's prisons.

Sandy said, 'It takes time to come to grips with what happened. I commanded troops in Vietnam and worked in minefields and tunnels, but nothing can prepare you for this. At first I meditated to escape the pain and guilt, then I started hearing the girls' voices crying to me, saying, "It's alright, Dad. We're happy. It was time for us to go". I managed to get 20 to 30 minutes to myself each day and gradually became able to release my stress, my grief—to be able to change things, to let go of the hate, to ultimately develop inner peace, to go for acceptance and forgiveness'.

Sandy sees his family's tragedy as being a catalyst that threw him into an entirely different belief system. He has studied relaxation and mind control in the United States and Australia. Sandy once said, 'My mission is to tell people that they have enormous power within them, and to teach them how to tap that power. I feel it is my responsibility to teach others how to develop this crucial life skill'.

He now travels the country teaching people of all ages and from all walks of life: he teaches accelerated learning and stress release techniques to children from six years old through to adults, holding classes in schools where he often brings together teachers, parents and Year 12 students. Importantly, students are encouraged to understand each others' needs.

If you still feel doubtful about the power of energy, think of it another way. Many of us have walked into a room and sensed the atmosphere, or walked into work and thought of the boss, 'He's in a bad mood', even before you have spoken to him. It's all the same thing.

Changing your energy levels

Like most things in life, we have the power within us to change our energy levels, so that we can attract abundance into our lives. You can change your energy levels by doing any of the following on a regular basis.

Energy responds to our thoughts. The more positive you are, the more you will lift your energy level. You can make a decision to be more positive, and surround yourself with inspirational material and mix with positive people but, in order to create long-lasting results, you need to build a history of success.

If you're living on an income of $40,000, don't plan to make a million in a year—you'll probably set yourself up for failure. One woman who attended my course trebled her income over eighteen months, but she did it one step at a time. At the time that I met Libby, she was a reasonably paid employee but she wanted a lot more money. She decided that she wanted to be self-employed but couldn't afford to take the risk of giving up financial security to start out on her own. She focused on what she wanted and visualised daily. Within weeks she was offered a six month assignment that paid more than her salary, and she only had to work three days a week. This gave her two free days a week plus more money to develop her business.

Small successes give us the opportunity to develop a positive expectancy. As our expectancy increases, so does the level of our vibrations. Our thoughts and feelings cause our energy to flow out into the world and other people respond. We can literally draw people into our lives to assist us in achieving our desires.

Energy responds to beauty. We often escape, or think of escaping, to the seaside, the mountains or countryside in order to recharge our batteries. We instinctively know that getting back to nature is good for us, and we respond to our surroundings as well. Do you sometimes feel melancholy on dark winter days? If you do, you're probably affected by SAD (Seasonal Affective Disorder) which was only discovered in the eighties. Lack of bright light affects some people greatly, so that they suffer from energy loss, depression and poor concentration. I've known from an early age that I could never live in the inner-city. I need to be able to look out the window and see the grass, sky and trees; I need to hear the birds, and I have an abundance of them in my garden. For me, these things signify beauty and lift my spirits. For you, it may be something else. Remember, beauty is in the eye of the beholder.

Energy responds to motion. Most people know that if you are feeling tired and washed out the best way to recharge is to do some exercise. If you want to change your emotional state, do something. Take a walk, do two minutes of exercises, look up at the sky or have a glass of water. Movement changes your emotional state. If you want to change the energy state of another person get them to move as well. If this is not possible, move yourself and you will find their response changes.

Energy responds to breathing. When I first started doing public speaking, I learnt how to use my breath. If you feel uptight and your voice starts to shake, take a deep breath. Deep controlled breathing can change you from feeling apprehensive to feeling calm. Just trying feeling anxious while taking deep breaths—it's impossible.

If you have two minutes to spare, do the exercise I mentioned earlier. Breathe in slowly to the count of four, hold your breath to the count of four, breathe out slowly to the count of four and then pause to the count of four. Meditate at least once a day and focus on your breathing. When you are in a meditative state your energy levels change.

SEND YOUR ENERGY AHEAD OF YOU

At one time, I was having a problem getting building plans approved by my local council. There was one building inspector, a most surly and uncommunicative man, who went out of his way to make things difficult. I rang every few days, I tried everything I knew to get my plans passed, but to no avail.

One day, when I had to deliver some more papers to this inspector, I decided to do something different. I sat in my car and changed the way I thought about him. I realised that to be that surly and uncooperative he couldn't be a very happy man, so I decided to be nice to him, no matter what. Before getting out of my car, I decided to send love to this man. I imagined a light coming into my head (from a higher power), exiting through my heart and connecting with him. I then went in to see him. For the first time he smiled at me, and my plans were approved the very next day.

You can change your state and those around you by practising how to use this power, or you can choose to stay the same.

Sandy MacGregor tells a story in his book, *Piece of Mind*[18] about how monkeys are caught by the natives of the Amazon basin.

They use a coconut, a piece of string and a peanut. One end of the coconut is cut open and a peanut is put inside. The other end is tied to a piece of string. The monkey is attracted to the moving coconut, spies the peanut inside, puts a hand into the coconut and fastens onto the peanut. The hand is now a fist, firmly grasping the peanut. However it is bigger than the opening of the coconut. The monkeys go crazy dancing around to shake off the coconut. They stomp on it and hit it against their head, all to no avail. Do they let go of the peanut? No! In fact the monkey gets caught and gives up its life rather than let go of the peanut.

How many peanuts do you hold onto? How much do you resist the idea that you cannot have the things that you desire?

SUMMARY

Our body acts an aerial that transmits and receives messages.

Your thoughts dictate what level you tune into—fear or abundance. Think about what you want.

Take regular short breaks to relax so that you can pick up messages being sent to you.

Listen to your intuition.

NOTES

CHAPTER NINE

HOW TO CREATE PERMANENT CHANGE

*The ancestor of every
action is a thought.*

Ralph Waldo Emerson

*Be prepared.
If you want to change
a deep-seated pattern,
it may take time
and effort initially,
but the end result
is worth the effort.*

There are times when you think you have something mastered, you've studied and you've applied all the principles, then something out of the ordinary happens and you find yourself responding in the same old way. Don't start blaming yourself or give up your dream; it is just a natural neurological response that needs to be changed.

Stimulus/Response

Do you remember the experiment carried out by Dr Ivan Pavlov? Pavlov placed a plate of food where his dogs could see it and smell it, but not reach it. Soon the dogs, feeling hungry, began salivating. After a while Pavlov rang a bell. A neurological connection was made: after Pavlov repeated this experiment a number of times, his dogs would begin salivating whenever they heard the bell, even though there was no food in front of them. We all respond to certain stimuli positively or negatively, just like Pavlov's dogs.

Can you recall a song that brings back memories? A girlfriend once told me that the song 'Rainy days and Mondays' always reminded her of me. I never hear that song now without remembering our conversation, even the exact location we were in when she made that comment. I never smell a cigar without being reminded of a boyfriend that I went out with who smoked cigars—30 years ago.

An event, a person, a feeling, an aroma, a place, even a voice tone, can trigger memories within us and we respond in a conditioned way. Perhaps when the day you set aside to look at your budget or financial situation arrives, you feel panic-stricken and avoid doing it. Maybe you were in a business that failed and now the thought of taking chances fills you with dread. You may be calm and confident in your everyday life but, when you go for a job interview, you feel like you are back at school. Or the sight of a bill fills you with so much fear that you bury the envelope unopened in a drawer. Perhaps whenever you start discussing money with your spouse, you start fighting. These are all perfectly normal scenarios that happen to millions of people. They are all responses to a given stimuli—when a certain situation happens, an automatic response takes place which means you keep on acting in the same old way.

Touch can stimulate a response. In his seminars, Tony Robbins uses, as an illustration a grief-stricken man at a funeral. The mourners who come up to express their sympathy touch him on the top part of the left-arm, we've all seen people do that. Years later, whenever anyone touches that man in that same spot, he can be overcome with feelings of grief, yet have no idea why.

Sound can stimulate a response. Not long after my son fell off the balcony the ambulance arrived, sirens blaring. They left with his body. For years, I could not hear the sound of sirens without shuddering and feeling immense pain.

Stories can be used to anchor a response. I use stories to anchor memories and positive emotions. If, throughout this book, I just told you that you have a choice in every situation, you would probably have read the words and moved on. Within a day, you would have forgotten all that I have said. By using stories such as Mitchell's accidents and the death of my son to illustrate a point, you are more likely to remember it because you probably felt some emotion while reading it. You may have even stopped to think how you would feel if the same thing happened to you. You will remember the point I was making, and there may come a time in your life when that memory will remind you that you have a choice. That is how we use anchors.

I have made a habit of taking all of the events of my life and anchoring them in happy memories; I decided to use the difficult times as examples to influence others to make positive changes. Now I can talk about my son's death because I no longer associate it with pain, I see it as the starting point of my life's work. By doing this, I not only help others but I found peace and happiness within myself.

A woman who attended my seminar said, 'I feel sorry for you but I don't agree with what you are saying, because you are using a form of hypnosis to change reality'. We are being conditioned every day by the media and the negative phrases that we hear over and over again from everyone around us. I don't see any merit in being miserable.

We respond to places, as well. If you have a job that you don't like, your feelings about the day may change the moment you walk into the building. You may have been feeling cheerful when you first woke up and carried that feeling with you as you travelled to work. However, chances are that the moment you saw the building your automatic response associated with that work—be it frustration or depression—took over. The building itself had no power over you, but your mind associated it with work that you don't like, so it acted as a stimuli and you went into an automatic response.

How to change your response

Many clients have left my office after a financial consultation and said how great they felt. A friend said that I had 'a gift' for making people feel good; no matter when she talks to me, she always feels better afterwards. I tell people that they can have what they want and that makes them feel good, and they associate that feeling with me.

So, how do we change our responses? One thing that influences your response is the intensity of your emotions at the time. The stronger the emotion, the stronger your response. A simple and quick way to change depression is to change your body language. Observe how you sit, walk and talk when you feel depressed. Shoulders slump, voice level drops, the energy drains and movement is slow. So, do the opposite. Smile, stand tall, put more energy into your voice and you will find it impossible to be depressed while you do this. It is a physical impossibility to be depressed while you smile.

Try this simple exercise. Think of a time that was absolutely wonderful in your life, a peak experience. Think of another time when you felt totally confident and duplicate the body language and breathing rhythms you experienced at that time. Place these experiences in your right hand, retain the feelings you associate with them and do some action with your right hand. Americans have a great habit of punching the sky and saying 'Yes' when something good happens. You may want to duplicate that, or do something that is meaningful to you. Do it again: if you have anchored correctly, you should feel confident and wonderful when you repeat that action. If not, try it again and remember to bring in the emotion of the peak experience; repeat the exercise about six times to ensure an association is made. Whenever you need this feeling in the future you can repeat this action and you will recall that feeling of happiness and confidence.

Tony Robbins has a practice at his seminars of getting his audience to bring their right arms across their bodies in a powerful fist and shout 'Yes'. He obviously waits until he has his audience in exactly the mood he wants, then throughout the day, as attention wanes, he gets everyone to stand and repeat that action. It's incredible to see thousands of people come to life when they do it.

Open your right hand again and remember those great feelings. Now turn your focus to your left hand. Place in that hand whatever negative experience about money you want to eliminate—perhaps you feel overwhelmed by financial problems, or money is a cause of arguments. Simply place the negative emotion and experience there. Then turn your attention back to your right hand. Remember the emotion, remember the power of that peak experience and go back to the stance you were in when you placed that positive experience in your right hand. Breathe the way you do when you feel powerful. Now place your open right palm on top of your open left palm. Imagine all the joy and confidence you feel filtering into your left palm and washing all negative memories away. You may need to repeat this five or six times. At first, you may need to repeat this exercise each time you find yourself reacting to another conditioned response but it won't be long before your positive response becomes automatic.

Anchoring is a very powerful technique. If you feel that you need help with this I suggest that you consult an NLP practitioner (a contact number is listed in the back of the book in the resource directory). NLP was discovered by John Grinder, a linguist, and Richard Bandler, a mathematician, Gestalt therapist and computer expert. Grinder and Bandler decided to seek people who were the best at what they do and model their behaviour. They discovered a unique system for creating change which they describe in their book entitled *Frogs into Princes*[16]. Their success has been phenomenal, with many of the world's leading motivational speakers, such as Tony Robbins, using the techniques that were developed. Therapists found that phobias that once took years to cure could now be cured in one session, using NLP techniques.

If you are not getting the results you desire in your life, remember you can change your responses. Our present is the result of our past conditioning—you have the power to change that conditioning to support your present and future choices.

SUMMARY

We all respond positively or negatively to specific stimuli.

Positive anchors can change our responses to any situation.

NOTES

CHAPTER TEN

HOW TO LIVE YOUR DREAM

If you want to win—you have to settle one thing right now. It doesn't matter how many times you have failed in the past. What matters is carving tiny footholds of success and remembering, reinforcing, and dwelling upon those footholds.

Denis Waitley

*Y*our level of
expectation
has a lot to do
with your success.
People with
high expectations
attract countless
opportunities.

We learn by repetition. To derive the greatest benefit from this book, read it many times, or pick it up, ask for guidance, and then open the page. Now is the time to put all that you have learnt into action.

What income bracket do you need to be in to achieve your dreams? If you earn $50,000 a year and you want a million-dollar-home and lifestyle, you may need to reassess your career. What type of work can you do that will provide that lifestyle? Some people win the lottery but are you prepared to put your dreams on hold for a 'maybe'? I'm not. I have seen many people fantasize about what they want, but they are not prepared to do anything to bring it into reality. Do you want your dream enough to work for it?

Have you worked out your moving towards' values, your 'moving away' from values and the rules you live by? Success can come easily and effortlessly but there are some things you have to know about yourself first. It's worth taking the time to get really clear on what you want. I have met people who have decided to follow a particular career path, not because it's what they want to do, but because they can't think of anything else. If they devoted the same amount of time to researching what they really wanted to do, rather than studying something they don't want to do, they would achieve more.

You may not be able to decide what you want straight away. It may take a week, a month or even a year, but it's worthwhile taking a year to discover what's important rather than spending 20 or 30 years doing something you dislike. How much time would you spend planning a year-long overseas trip? I imagine it would take quite a while. Your future deserves the same amount of time and effort.

Possibly you already know what you want, but still don't have it. What do you need to do to start things happening? Check how much of your day is spent focusing on what you want. If you are really honest with yourself, you may find that a large proportion of your time is wasted energy thinking about what you don't have.

Putting it into practice

Not everyone achieves goals in the same way. How we achieve our goals depends on our beliefs, values and rules we live by. I think this is where many people come unstuck—they try a method because it works for someone else and when it doesn't work for them, they give up. You may achieve relationship goals in one way and money goals in a different way; it doesn't really matter it's the end result that counts.

Some people need to take practical steps, by breaking their goals into small components and achieving them through traditional channels, like saving for what they want. If this is the method you prefer, read on.

The traditional approach

Write down what you want. Decide what you want to achieve within the next 12 month, five years, 10 years, and over the course of your lifetime.

Take practical steps. Remember your words and actions must support your goal at all times. If you want to be self-employed, look for ways to increase your knowledge. If you want to make money through investments, allocate a set amount to your investment fund each payday.

Make a plan. Do something every week that will take you closer to your goal. It may be reading, attending seminars or courses, joining a networking group or studying interior decorating so you can decorate your dream home. Consult a financial adviser and make a financial plan. You may want to say affirmations and visualise yourself as having achieved your goal.

Celebrate your successes. Do something special for yourself each time you achieve a goal no matter how small. You need to recognise and acknowledge all of your achievements, and give yourself credit where it is due.

Most people can have a far more affluent lifestyle simply by learning how to manage and invest money; some need to take practical steps otherwise they cannot mentally accept that they can have what they want. This method has worked for me for small goals, and most people need to start out this way so they have some history of succeeding. However, I have not achieved any of my major lifetime goals in the traditional way.

MY WAY

Many people say it is impossible to achieve certain goals and, if you follow the traditional approach, it is. For instance, imagine a couple who are in their fifties who want to buy a home but have no savings (maybe they lost their home and assets in a previous business). Most lending institutions would lend them money over, say, a 12-year period, but trying to repay $200-300,000 over that time frame is, for most people impossible. If, on top of that, this couple had a poor credit history because of their failed business, they would probably have to wait another five years before they could obtain a loan anyway.

This is how most people think. Most people believe we can

only achieve goals in traditional ways, but it is precisely those beliefs that limit the choices they make. Because of the life path that I have chosen, I didn't have a lot of options open to me I had no way of achieving my goals by traditional methods, so I discovered alternative ways. The methods I use as I grow and evolve may differ but I get the same results. When I don't get the results I want there is usually something more for me to learn, or I realise I am meant to travel down a different path. I decided a number of years ago that I am not in this world by accident, I am here to learn specific lessons personally and to share what I learn with others. Here is how I achieve my goals:

1. I spend time to become very clear in my mind about what I want.

2. I put out for what I want.

3. I meditate on what I want, but let the universe take care of the details.

4. I give what I want to receive.

5. I take action when it feels right in my body.

Some people who prefer life to be more complicated may dismiss this method as being too simplistic. It's not really that easy because, in order to be very clear on what you want, you have to do all that work on yourself. Assuming you have done that, however, you learn to attract what you need to you (this I covered in Chapters Three and Eight).

One reader told me she was browsing through a bookshop when my book, *Financially Free*, fell off the shelf and hit her on the head. Another just happened to be feeling down about money one day and walked into a newsagent and there was my book. She later attended my seminar and we became friends—was it coincidence? Is it just chance that at this time in my life I have the insight and desire to write the words that you need to read? It's all a part of the pattern of life. Everything that we need is already there for us; all you have to do is put out the thought, and you can draw all that you need to you.

I meditate twice a day, usually for 10 to 20 minutes, depending on my commitments. I focus on my breathing, I don't need music, mantras or anything special. Some days, I can't remember anything about my meditation (that's when I have slipped into the gap). Dr Deepak Chopra describes the 'gap' as the space between our thoughts, where there is no mental activity. So many people give up on meditation because they cannot still their minds, all you have to do is slow down the thinking process. I have found it easier to meditate since I have used this method, but some days it's harder to still the thoughts that circulate in my mind. I don't worry about it, I just flow with what is happening. While meditating I have a very clear intention of what I want, but I let the universe decide how I'm going to achieve it. Like anything practice makes perfect—the more you do it, the easier it gets. It is addictive but, unlike other addictions this one won't harm you, it will make your life richer.

I believe that we get back in life what we give out. If you want love, you give love, if you want money, you give money. I have recently made a change to my twice-daily meditations: one I use as a giving, so my clear intention during the meditation is to spread love and prosperity to others; the second meditation is my receiving, where my intention is to receive the desires of my heart.

The very first day I changed the pattern in my meditation and started giving, I received a phone call from a woman who is a member of my local barter group (a barter group is where you exchange goods and services with each other rather than use cash). At the time, I happened to be several hundreds of dollars in debt to this club and was wondering how I could clear my account quickly so that I could use it for something else I wanted. The woman who rang me had moved and was not renewing her membership, but she still had several hundreds of dollars of credit. She said she would like to transfer the credit balance from her account to me as a gift. In return, she asked if I could help someone who may need advice but could not afford to pay. I asked and I received, in a totally unexpected way.

I follow my intuition. If I feel I should start, not knowing where the money is coming from, I do. If it doesn't feel right, I wait for a clearer indication. If I step out in faith, then I have to be prepared for the consequences if things don't go the way I planned. You need always to accept responsibility for your actions. As you take charge of your life, you empower yourself and others. As you discover riches, you enrich others. As you share your knowledge and love, you touch people around you. How often do we get so caught up in our everyday cares that we overlook the important things in life?

Sometimes you may feel guilty for concentrating so much on money, but money is important, too. Money is a wonderful commodity that can ease your worries, provide an affluent lifestyle, and create beauty. Having the money that you want gives you the freedom to focus on the important things in life, but it's not everything, either.

One day I was feeling harassed after an unusually hectic week. I had been racing to meet deadlines every day. I was waiting for plans to be approved by council so building work could commence on my home. My car was in the smash repairers, so I didn't have transport, the cat was sick, I couldn't get to the bank and I had no money, and my hairdresser cut layers in my hair after it took a year to grow them out. I'm sure you know those days, we've all had them!

Just when I was feeling totally frazzled and wanted some time out for myself, my youngest kept demanding attention. Unfortunately I let off steam. I yelled rather loud and long.

Did I damage my children? My eldest daughter laughed and said, 'Do you realise you're yelling again. It sounds awful'. Laura didn't get perturbed—she just kept on demanding my attention until she got it. I was still cranky when I went to bed.

When I woke the next morning Laura, who was only five at that time, had left me a note on my bedside table. It read:

I love you Anne
I love you.

It's not the big things in life, it's the little things that make life worthwhile. Fame and fortune and the achievement of goals can be great fun, but life is really about love. Learning to love ourselves and each other. Reaching for a dream is about finding love, for love is all there is.

Strive for balance. Give yourself permission to do work that you love and be paid abundantly for it. Don't put off important things like spending time with people you love until you have everything you want, otherwise it will never happen. Self-knowledge is the key to change and the pathway to prosperity. Acting on that knowledge will open the doors of abundance for you.

At the end of this book, I've included information on the books, courses, and services provided by the many people whose stories I've shared with you, as well as information on the services that I provide. I hope you will write and share your success stories with me. If you are happy for me to share your story with others, please let me know. Even if we never meet, I hope that I have helped you on your journey.

I hope you gained as much from this book as I have learnt about myself through the process of writing it. I started out with a title, and a very strong feeling that I should write it—that's all. Now, less than a month later, it is complete. And they told me I could never write. When you are doing what you are meant to be doing, things flow. Victor Hugo once said, 'There is nothing more powerful than a dream whose time has come'.

It is your time now, time to dream, time to plan, time to take action. Remember, though, that success is what you perceive it to be. My definition of success is being the person you want to be, and living the life you want. Remember always that you have your desires for a reason; when you do not have what you want, you are going against the universe's plan for you. We are here on the planet to learn how to love and when you love yourself, you fulfil your own desires.

May your life be full of joy, abundance and love.

MORE FROM

ANNE HARTLEY

COURSE FACILITATORS

Franchise opportunities exist for a select number of people to conduct Anne Hartley's courses. Full-training, referrals and support provided, and only one facilitator per state is appointed. You need communication skills, a belief in the programs, teaching abilities, to be able to organise and promote courses, and have funds available for franchise fee and start-up costs.

Contact Anne Hartley for more information.
    Ph/Fax: (02) 9971 2083.

THE PSYCHOLOGY OF MONEY HOME-STUDY PROGRAM

Success doesn't just happen, in order to create the life you want, you need to study success. This powerful home-study program could change the way you think about and handle money forever. The program contains four cassettes by Anne Hartley, plus lesson notes and exercises. The program is designed to be completed over 30 days, but you can work at your own pace.

Cost: $95

Available only by mail order. Please forward your cheque or credit card details (Visa/Bankcard/Mastercard) to:

Hart Publishing Pty Ltd
PO Box 816
Brookvale NSW 2100
Australia
Ph/Fax: (02) 9971 2083

FINANCIALLY FREE
THINK RICH TO BE RICH

(A woman's guide to creating wealth)

by Anne Hartley

- Change your attitudes
- Change your habits
- Expand your horizons
- Create wealth

If you want to be rich don't deprive yourself, do pamper yourself, live prosperously now and plan for an affluent future.

Anne Hartley has helped thousand of women and couples to become wealthy.

Published by Doubleday

Cost: $17.95 (includes postage)

Available in bookshops or by mail order. Please forward your cheque or credit card details (Visa/Bankcard/Mastercard) to:

    Hart Publishing Pty Ltd
    PO Box 816
    Brookvale NSW 2100
    Australia
    Ph/Fax: (02) 9971 2083

FINANCIALLY FREE HOME-STUDY PROGRAM

The material in this program is the same as if you attended a four week course with Anne Hartley. When you purchase the program you will receive four cassettes, lesson notes and exercises that will assist you in achieving your dreams.

Cost: $95

Available only by mail order. Please forward your cheque or credit card details (Visa/Bankcard/Mastercard) to:

Hart Publishing Pty Ltd
PO Box 816
Brookvale NSW 2100
Australia
Ph/Fax: (02) 9971 2083

DEBT FREE

HOW TO GET OUT OF DEBT, STAY OUT OF DEBT, AND STILL LIVE THE LIFE YOU WANT.

by Anne Hartley

This book is about change—changing the way we spend and the way we manage money. Debt Free provides practical, hands-on activities and planning sheets to help you create an organised system to manage your money and eliminate your debt. It shows you how to get out of difficulties, negotiate with creditors, understand your rights and change the conditions that got you into debt in the first place.

Discover how to achieve real prosperity—not just the illusion.

Cost: $17.95 (including postage)

Published by Doubleday. Available from bookshops or by mail order. Please forward your cheque or credit card details (Visa/Bankcard/Mastercard) to:

    Hart Publishing Pty Ltd
    PO Box 816
    Brookvale NSW 2100
    Australia
    Ph/Fax: (02) 9971 2083

POSITIVE PEOPLE

'Positive People' is Anne Hartley's bi-monthly newsletter full of inspirational stories about people who are living their dreams. Guaranteed to lift your spirits and keep you motivated. Available only by subscription.

$15 for three issues, or $30 for six issues.

Please forward your cheque or credit card details (Visa/Bankcard/Mastercard) to:

    Hart Publishing Pty Ltd
    PO Box 816
    Brookvale NSW 2100
    Australia
    Ph/Fax: (02) 9971 2083

DIRECTORY
OF CONTRIBUTORS

Throughout this book I have told many inspirational stories, which have been taken from books that I have read and been inspired by. These are acknowledged in the Reference Section. Others were contributed by professional speakers or come from interviews that I have done for my newsletter 'Positive People'.

Information on the services provided by some of the contributors is listed here in alphabetical order.

Directory of Contributors

Steve Alexander.   Steve founded a company called Success 2000 Pty Ltd, that provides a range of consulting services specialising in helping people achieve more through enhanced performance. He has studied behavioural psychology, philosophy, physiology, quantum physics, neurology, meditation, body energy and the relationship between thought and health. He has accreditation in identification and correction of dyslexic conditions, and is a professionally qualified applied kinesiologist and has a Diploma in Clinical Kinesiology. He can be contacted at PO Box 662, Chatswood, NSW 2057. Telephone: (02) 9959 4652. Fax: (02) 9923 2428.

June Archer.   Happy Feet, the foot exercising program, can be ordered from June for just $A20. If purchasing from overseas, please add on postage. June is also a licensed leader of the Financially Free program. She can be contacted at PO Box 224, Laidley, QLD 4341.

Wayne Berry. — Top Gun Business Academy was created by Wayne Berry in 1991 and uses ultra-high speed learning technology and Neuro-Linguistic Programming technology to produce outstanding increases in sales results. For further details, contact Wayne Berry at Top Gun Business Academy, 2 Chamberlain's Lane, VIC 3191. Telephone: (03) 9521 0500. Fax: (03) 9521 0499.

Sue Boult. — Sue and Adrian Boult provide bed-and-breakfast accommodation in individual chalets set on nine acres just half-an-hour outside central Auckland. For more information contact Sue or Adrian Boult, PO Box 227, Silverdale, Hibiscus Coast, New Zealand.

Jack Canfield. — Jack is the President of Self-Esteem Seminars and The Canfield Training Group, a seminar and training company dedicated to assisting individuals and organisations to live in alignment with their highest purpose and aspirations. Jack conducts in-house trainings for corporations, government agencies and school districts and public seminars for individuals. He also delivers keynote speeches for state regional and national conferences and conventions.

Jack also has a wide variety of books, audio cassette and video cassette programs available. If you would like to receive a brochure or discuss a possible workshop or speaking date, please contact him by calling US (310) 337 9222 or 1-800-2-ESTEEM, or write to 6035 Bristol Parkway, Culver City, California 90230, USA.

Burt Dubin. is the developer of the Speaking Success System, a powerful instrument for helping aspiring and professional speakers position, package, promote, and present themselves. "You are a master—an absolute master—I recommend your System without reservation," says Joe J Charbonneau, CSP, CPAE. Burt may be reached at Personal Achievement Institute, 1 Speaking Success Road, Kingman, Arizona 86402-6543 or call 800-321-1225. (Worldwide E-mail: BDUBINSPKR @aol.com)

Peter Fortune.

Peter is renowned for his ability to make people laugh. Peter believes that what people commit themselves to they will achieve—along with the tools to do it. Peter is highly in demand as a speaker and can be booked through Ovations International Speakers Bureau, Henry Lawson Business Centre, Birkenhead Point, NSW 2047. Telephone: (02) 819 6377. Fax: (02) 719 1294. If you would like to order Peter's book *The Easy Guide to Public Speaking*, you can contact him direct at P O Box 362, Strawberry Hills, NSW 2012. Telephone: (02) 9982 5058.

Rick Gelinas.

Rick is the President of the Lucky Acorns Delphi Foundation in Miami, Florida. He is a master educator and has dedicated his life to making a difference to children. You can reach him at 5888 S.W. 77 Terrace, Miami, Florida, USA or call (305) 667 7756.

Mark Victor Hansen.

Mark has spent a lifetime dedicated to his mission to make a profound and positive difference in peoples' lives. His book *Future Diary* is read by thousands across the country.

Dare to Win, his latest book, has been highly endorsed by Norman Vincent Peale and Og Mandino, both legends in the area of personal development. In addition, he has written *How to Achieve Total Prosperity* and the *Miracle of Tithing*, all best-sellers.

Mark is a big man with a big heart and a big spirit, an inspiration to all who seek to better themselves. You can contact Mark by calling USA (714) 759 9304 or write to 6035 Bristol Parkway, Culver City, California 90230, USA.

Tad James.

Tad James is a recognised leader in the dynamic field of accelerated human growth and change. He has a masters' degree in communications and a PhD in Ericksonian hypnosis. As a practising therapist and Certified Master Trainer in Neuro-Linguistic Programming (NLP), Tad has created a powerful tool for change known as Time Line Therapy™. Tad is the author of *Time Line Therapy and the Basis of Personality*, and *The Secret of Creating your Future*. Tad is represented in Australia by

Universal Events,
PO Box 664, Bondi Junction,
NSW, 2022.
Telephone: (02) 369 4510.
Fax: (02) 369 5133.

Sandy MacGregor.

Sandy has received professional training and now teaches others how to access the power of the subconscious mind through books, tapes, seminars and talks to the public, educational and corporate sector. Sandy teaches both children and adults. Sandy is the author of *Piece of Mind*, and can be contacted through his company The CALM Office, 2/80 Chandos Street, Crows Nest, NSW 2065.
Telephone: (02) 439 7188.
Fax: (02) 439 7587.

Mitchell.

Mitchell, as he likes to be called, is an international speaker and author of *The Man Who Would Not be Defeated*. He is an incredible inspiration and is in great demand throughout the world, Mitchell is represented in Australia by Ovations International Speakers Bureau, 414 Henry Lawson Business Centre, Birkenhead Point,

NSW 2047.
Telephone: (02) 819 6377.
Fax: (02) 719 1294.

Pam Mountfield.

Pam is a qualified naturopath, specialised kinesiologist, herbalist, hypnotherapist and masseuse. In her clinic, she combines kinesiology with naturopathy to work on many different types of issues including stress management, health, dyslexia, sports performance and emotional stress release. Pam also teaches various kinesiology courses, 'Touch for Health' and 'One Brain' series. She can be contacted at The Infinite Potential Centre, 414 Sydney Road, Balgowlah, NSW 2095. Telephone: (02) 9949 7819. Fax: (02) 9948 3820.

Tony Robbins.

Tony is represented in Australia by Sales Pursuit. For information on his seminars and materials contact Sales Pursuit Results Pty Ltd, 580 Harris Street, Ultimo. NSW 2007. Telephone: (02) 281 8177.

Jim Rohn.	Jim is an entrepreneur, businessman and trusted adviser to business, government and educational leaders. He has addressed over three million people worldwide. For more information on Jim's seminars, books, tapes and videos contact, Jim Rohn International, 9810 North MacArthur Boulevard, Suite 303, Irving, Texas 75063 USA Telephone: (214) 401 1000. Fax: (214) 401 2003.
Barbara and Terry Tebo.	Barbara and Terry are personal development teachers, corporate trainers, counsellors and authors. Through their company 'Lifespring', they teach their popular 'Free to be Me' seminars in Sydney and wherever people invite them to come. 'Free to be Me' is also available as a correspondence course using audio-tapes, course notes and the guidance of a personal tutor. Their book, also entitled *Free to be Me*, is about relationships and feelings and is published by Bantam. For more information on their work write to: Lifespring, 113 Campbell Drive, Wahroonga NSW, 2076.

Directory of Contributors

	Telephone: (02) 489 5001. Fax: (02) 490 4119.
Tommy Tighe.	To purchase Tommy's bumper stickers write to Tommy Tighe, 17283 Ward Street, Fountain Valley, CA 92708, U S A The sticker costs $US3; please allow for postage outside of the U.S.
Dottie Walters.	Dottie publishes many products and publications in the field of sales and professional speaking. To obtain a free gift copy of her catalogue, write to PO Box 1120, Glendora, CA, USA 91740. Fax: (818) 335 6127.
NLP and Time Line Therapy™.	If you would like to consult with an NLP and.or Time Line Practitioner in your local area contact Neuroads Pty Ltd, c/- PO Box 517, Mona Vale NSW 2103. Telephone/Fax: (02) 9918 3025
The Australian Kinesiology Association.	For more information on accredited Kinesiologists in all areas, contact PO Box 190, East Kew VIC 3102. Telephone: (03) 859 2254. Fax: (03) 859 2849.

REFERENCES AND RECOMMENDED READING

1. Robert Schuller, *You Can Become The Person You Want To Be*, Hawthorn Books, New York, 1973.

2. Dr Wayne W Dyer, *You'll See It When You Believe It*, Schwartz Publishing, Melbourne, 1989.

3. Dottie Walters, *The Greatest Speakers I ever Heard*, WRS Publishing, Texas, 1995.

4. Jack Canfield & Mark Victor Hansen, *Chicken Soup for the Soul*, Health Communications, Florida, 1993.

5. Jim Rohn, *Seven Strategies for Wealth and Happiness*, Brolga Publishing, Melbourne, 1986.

6. Charles Paul Conn, *The Possible Dream*, Horwitz, Sydney, 1977.

7. Anita Roddick, *Body and Soul*, Vermillion, London, 1992.

8. Anthony Robbins, *Awaken the Giant Within*, Simon & Schuster, New York, 1991.

9. David Jansen, *Full Circle: An Olympic champion shares his breakthrough story*, Random House, New York, 1994.

10. Gordon Stokes/Daniel Whiteside, *One Brain*, Three in One Concepts, Burbank, California, 1987.

References and Recommended Reading

11. W Mitchell, *The Man Who Would Not Be Defeated*, Brolga Publishing, Melbourne, 1995.

12. Louise Samways, *Your MindBody Energy*, Viking O'Neill, Ringwood, Victoria, 1992.

13. James Redfield and Carol Adrienne, *The Celestine Prophecy an Experiential Guide*, Bantam, Sydney, 1995.

14. Nancy Rosanoff, *Intuition Workout: A practical Guide to Discovering and Developing your Inner Knowing*, Aslan Publishing, California, 1988.

15. Deepak Chopra, *Quantum Healing*, Bantam, New York, 1989.

16. Richard Bandler and John Grinder, *Frogs into Princes*, Utah, 1979.

17. Thom Hunter, condensed from *Those-not-so-still small voices*, Nowpress, Colorado Springs, Colorado. Condensed story Reader's Digest, February, 1995.

18. Sandy MacGregor, *Piece of Mind*, Calm, Lindfield, Sydney, 1992.

Anne Hartley recommends subliminal tapes. Subliminal tapes are used to reprogram the subconscious mind, the source from which will flow all your future desires, abilities, drives, habits, fears and other limiting or empowering factors...consider subliminal tapes.

SUBLIMINAL TAPES

For over 10 years the SCWL technique Subliminal Tapes, by Midwest Research, have assisted thousands of people in Australia to achieve the success they want, be it prosperity, stress reduction, self confidence, weight loss, academic skills, sport, eradication of fears, anxiety or better health.

SCWL tapes have as many as 100 affirmations repeated nearly 1,000 times, each embedded within the relaxing sounds of ocean waves. These embedded affirmations are absorbed by your subconscious mind to replace your old thinking. A New You!

Let the SCWL subliminals focus and magnify the latent power of your subconscious to effortlessly transform you to achieve whatever you want. Use subliminal tapes while you study, read, work, play or sleep.

OVER 100 TITLES TO CHOOSE FROM

All SCWL programs come with a 90 day results guarantee.

A special free tapes offer for all purchasers.
Mention you saw the ad in Anne's book.
Buy 3 tapes, pick 1 more free = 4 tapes
Buy 6 tapes, pick 6 more free = 12 tapes

SUBLIMINAL TAPES

Our tapes include the following topics
Concentration, Memory & Study Skills
Communication & Relationships
Feeling Better & Being Positive
Weight Loss & Better Health
Improving Natural Abilities
Confidence & Self Image
Sporting Mental Edge
Motivation & Attitude
Relaxation & Stress
Personal Growth
Fears & Phobias
Breaking Habits

David Murphy
MidWest Research SCWL

P.O. Box 502,
St Leonards NSW 2065

Telephone: (02) 9906 2790
Toll Free: 1800 655 374
Mobile: 0414 608043

"Ring for a free brochure"